BAKERY AND CONFECTIONERY

CHEF SATHISHKUMAR SOMASUNDARAM

Made with ♥ on the Notion Press Platform
www.notionpress.com

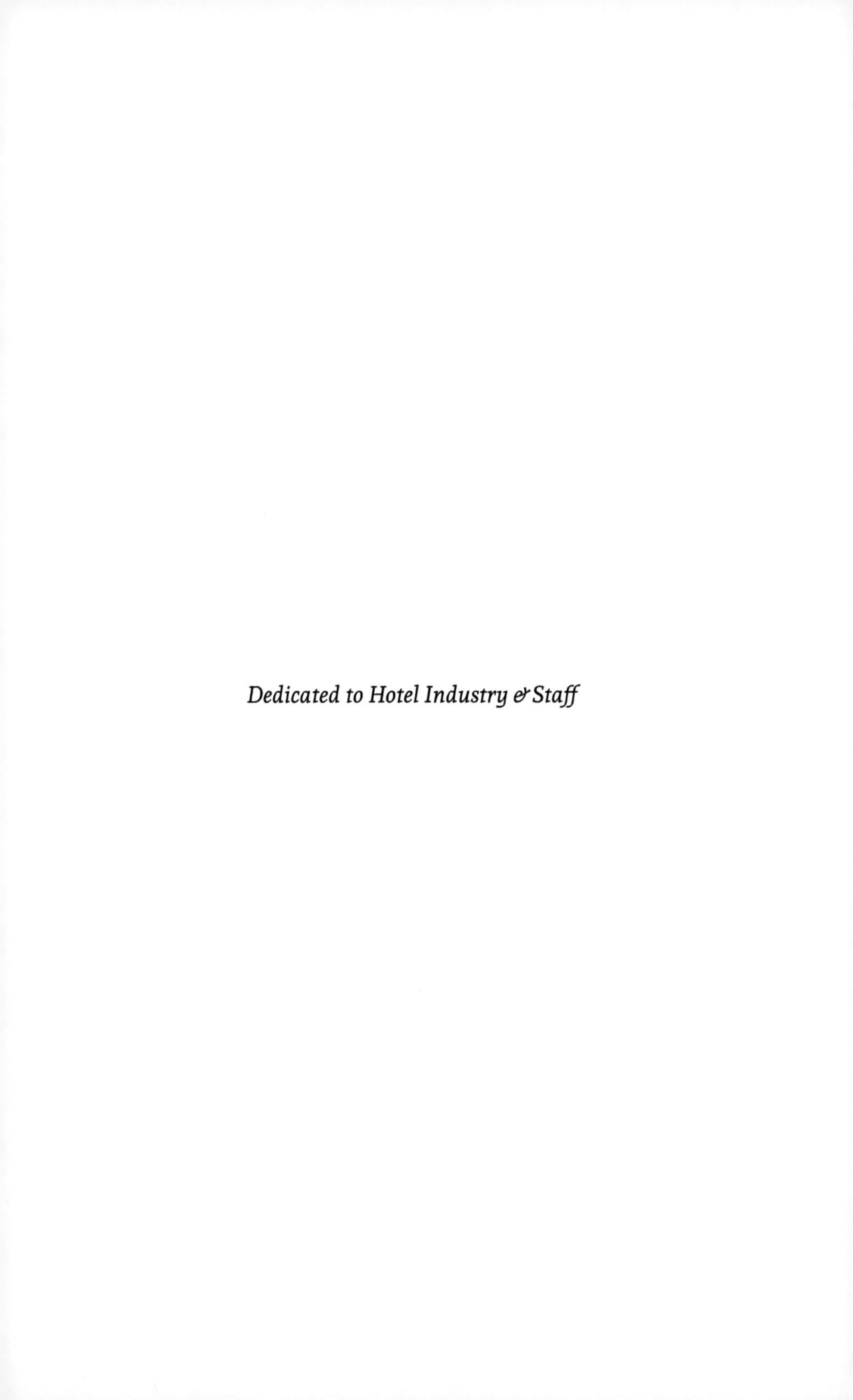

Dedicated to Hotel Industry & Staff

Contents

FOREWORD

This book provides a widely useful compilation of ideas, cases, innovative approaches, and practical strategies for enhancing a little-discussed school activit Bakery . By taking a new look at these ubiquitous programs, Anne Turn Baugh Lockwood identifies a substantial resource in the effort to increase student learning. In this book he provides an enormously useful range of strategies for designing, implementing, and evaluating Food Safety in Kitchen. This work would be an important resource if it only highlighted the ways Bakery , could enrich their missions by establishing academics as a more central part of their work. But the book goes well beyond just making us aware of this seemingly underutilized learning setting. It covers and describes all the major factors in building successful Food Safety in Kitchen that enhance achievement. This volume is an important resource for school principals, agencies that provide Food Safety in Kitchen, districts, and parent groups whose children use these services. First, it provides a new perspective on Food Safety in Kitchen, showing how they can be an important source for both recreation and academic learning. Food Safety in Kitchen is found all across the United States serving millions of students. Understanding how they can more effectively serve the learning needs of students adds a major cache of time for helping all students achieve. In another section, Lockwood lists an important set of issues to consider when designing an afterschool program and then adds an inventory of important questions to consider. She describes barriers to success and then presents suggestions for overcoming those barriers. Throughout the book, Lockwood sets out to make the material accessible to readers interested in implementing these programs—these ideas are found in the form of questions and suggestions, tables of issues to address, and practical strategies to consider. The tables and strategies themselves are worth the price of the book. This book also examines several other issues that often spell the end of quality programs—developing a parent and community base of support, designing adequate program evaluation processes, and planning for sustainability. One finds a useful set of questions, ideas, and strategies for building a base of support among parents and the community. The section on program evaluation is quite practical and detailed. It offers a clear description of ways schools can and should evaluate Bakery. Finally, the book on sustainability details challenges to the viability of Food Safety in Kitchen and suggests actions should take to ensure that these programs are successful in the long term. Overall, this book offers a variety of hotel and Food leaders a concrete, useful, and in-depth look at ways to design, implement, and evaluate a major resource in the learning of students. Clearly written, well organized, and enormously practical, it should be in every chef's professional library.

Chef Sathishkumar Somasundaram
Assistant Professor
Department of Catering Science and Hotel Management
Nehru Arts and Science Collage –Coimbatore
T.R Rajesh Pandian
Head of Department
Department of Catering Science and Hotel Management
Nehru Arts and Science Collage –Coimbatore

PREFACE

I realize that this book will create a great deal of Food handler. It has never been easy to challenge the consensus because the System – of any kind, in any context – will try to preserve the status quo, by all means possible. He spent 19 years in the field of hotel management as a chef. I feel obliged to share my knowledge, analyses, and conclusions. Hopefully, this book will raise the level of awareness among the general public and students initiate the discussion that, in turn, may entail major cultural changes, as well as a revision of the consumer basket. The beneficiaries will be all of us – ourselves, our children, our beloved ones, and the society, as a whole – who will live a healthier, and longer, life. I would like the food consumption to be not a routine procedure for gaining nutrients that the body needs, but a science-based process with complete predictability of its overall impact and fate of every food component entering the human body. Throughout, the book has been written with this audience in mind. At times, the science presented might seem overwhelming: busy schemes with multiple structures, electrons movements, charges, and intimidating chemical names. I hope that you won't be easily discouraged are very light in chemistry and can be easily understood by a layperson. One of the important features of this book is that it does not have a textbook structure when the chapters, the group of readers will be represented by professionals from the food industry, academia, and government agencies, as well as consumer protection. But I do hope that the information and knowledge presented will become a wake-up call for the general public, regulatory agencies, legislators, business leaders, coming to the realization that the current state of affairs is not satisfactory, to say the least, and it needs to be fixed .I hope this book is widely read. If we are to avoid the blunders of the past, then we need to change the direction and start benefiting from the knowledge base created by the food handler. We did not have this chance a decade ago. Now is the right time.

Acknowledgements

Like many authors who wrote about Food Safety in Kitchen before me, I want to express my thanks and admiration to the group of visionaries who invented Food Safety in Kitchen and to those who keep extending it creatively and applying it to new domains. I am very grateful to the many readers of the preliminary forms of the manuscript who taught me a lot by their criticism and suggested ideas that are now implemented in the text. I am also obliged to my students whose blank looks alerted me to inappropriate presentation strategies and whose improvements of classroom examples served to improve the text. I hope that I will get similar constructive suggestions for improvements from the readers of this book as well. Finally, I must acknowledge the influence of the Bakery. I learned a lot from it and borrowed some of the ideas expressed at this forum for examples and exercises. I have been teaching Food Safety for the last five years and forgotten many of the students who actively shaped my understanding of Bakery and influenced my teaching, I wish Thanks to Google.com and Fssai of India Also wish to thank the following Family and friends whose names stand out in my memory. Most of them are now employed as professional Food Safety in Kitchen programmers. Finally, but most importantly, I wish to thank my family. During the long time that it took to write this book, my wife Saranaya managed to pretend that spending the time that other people devote to holidays on my computer was a part of normal life, smoothed over my continuous swings between fascination and frustration with this book, and added a human dimension to my life. My two children - Ivan, Vishnu and Vishwa – helped greatly to maintain this illusion. I have been very lucky to have a family that provided such a warm, supportive, and stimulating environment.

I wish to thank my College and Management (NASC Family)
Nehru Arts and Scienece College - Coimbatore

Prologue

Food safety or Food hygiene is a scientific method & discipline that describes how to handle, prepare, and store food in order to avoid food-borne illness. A food-borne disease outbreak occurs when two or more cases of a similar illness occur as a result of the consumption of a common food. This includes a number of routines that must be followed in order to avoid potential health risks. As a result, food safety frequently overlaps with food defence to protect consumers. This line of thought has two tracks: safety between industry and market, and then safety between market and consumer. When it comes to market-to consumer practices, the common assumption is that food should be safe in the market, and the main concern is safe delivery and preparation of the food for the consumer. Food can transmit pathogens, which can cause illness or death in humans or other animals. Bacteria, viruses, mould, and fungus are the most common pathogens. Pathogens can use food as a growth and reproduction medium. Food preparation standards are intricate in developed countries, whereas less developed countries have fewer standards and less enforcement of those standards. or Food hygiene is a scientific method & discipline that describes how to handle, prepare, and store food in order to avoid food-borne illness. A food-borne disease outbreak occurs when two or more cases of a similar illness occur as a result of the consumption of a common food. This includes a number of routines that must be followed in order to avoid potential health risks. As a result, food safety frequently overlaps with food defence to protect consumers. This line of thought has two tracks: safety between industry and market, and then safety between market and consumer. When it comes to market-to consumer practices, the common assumption is that food should be safe in the market, and the main concern is safe delivery and preparation of the food for the consumer. Food can transmit pathogens, which can cause illness or death in humans or other animals. Bacteria, viruses, mould, and fungus are the most common pathogens. Pathogens can use food as a growth and reproduction medium. Food preparation standards are intricate in developed countries, whereas less developed countries have fewer standards and less enforcement of those standards.

I

General Information-Measuring Heat and Density

Chef on Bakery

General information-measuring Heat and Density, dough and cake mixing temperatures, yeast calculations, raw materials used in bakery and their role.

Measuring Tools

Conversion table :

1. **Conversion Formulas:**

When it is necessary to convert Fahrenheit temperature to Centigrade, the following may be used:

Fahrenheit – 32 X 5 / 9

When it is necessary to convert Centigrade to Fahrenheit temperature, the following may be used:

Centigrade X 9 / 5

2. **Volume Equivalents:**

Quantity

Equivalent

3 teaspoons

1 tablespoon

2 tablespoons
1 fl. Ounce
16 tablespoons (8 fl.ounces)
1 cup
2 cups (16 fl.ounces)
1 pint
2 pints (32 fl.ounces)
1 quart
4 quarts (128 fl.ounces)
1 gallon

3. Metric Conversion:

Weight
1 ounce = 28.35 grams
1 pound = 454 grams
1 gram = 0.035 ounces
1 kilogram = 2.2 pounds

A. to convert ounces to grams, multiply by 28.35
B. to convert grams to ounces, multiply by 0.03527
C. to convert kilogram to pounds, multiply by 2.2046
D. to convert pounds to kilogram, multiply by 0.4535924

4. Metric Conversions:

Volume
1 ounce = 29.57ml
1 cup = 2 dl, 2 cl, 7 ml (237 ml)
1 quart = 9 dl, 4 cl, 6 ml (946 ml)
1 milliliter = 0.034 fl.ounces
1 liter = 33.8 flounces

a. To convert quarts to liters, multiply by 0.946
b. To convert liters to quarts, multiply by 1.05625
c. To convert liters to pints, multiply by 2.1125
d. To convert liters to ounces, multiply by 33.8
e. To convert pints to liters, multiply by 0.473
f. To convert quarts to milliliters, multiply by 946
g. To convert milliliters to pints, multiply by 0.0021125
h. To convert milliliters to ounces multiply by 0.0338

5. Metric Conversion:

Length

1 inch = 25.4 mm

1 centimeter = 0.39 inches

1 meter – 39.4 inches

a. To convert inches to millimeters, multiply by 25.4

b. To convert inches to centimeters, multiply by 2.54

c. To convert millimeters to inches, multiply by 0.03937

d. To convert centimeters to inches, multiply by 0.3937

e. To convert meters to inches, multiply by 39.3701

Raw Materials:

In the bakery industry, the bakers prepare different varieties of cakes, biscuits, fermented products, sponge cakes, pastries and decorated cakes, etc.

To prepare the above product we mainly need some ingredients. These ingredients are called "Raw Materials". There are lots of ingredients that are used to prepare the products and these ingredients are classified into two types. They are

1. Essential ingredients

2. Optional ingredients

We cannot make any products without the essential ingredients. The optional ingredients on the other hand are added to improve the quality of the product.

Essential ingredients for bakery and confectionery products are

1. Flour

2. Sugar

3. Fat

4. Eggs

5. Yeast

6. Salt

7. Water

The optional ingredients are

1. **Milk and Milk Product**

2. **Dry fruits, Nuts**
3. **Fresh fruits**
4. **Flavours**
5. **Chemicals**
6. **Spices**
7. **Chocolates**
8. **Cocoa powder**
9. **Corn Flour**
10. **Mixed fruit jam**
11. **Custard powder**
12. **Setting materials**
13. **Colors**

In our bakery industry flour plays a major role. This flour is obtained from wheat. Wheat is the most important cereal among all grains. From quality wheat we can get quality flour. The Quality of Wheat depends upon the following conditions.

1. Soil
2. Quality of seeds
3. Climate
4. Manure
5. Farming Techniques
Wheat is classified in various methods such as

1. **Type**
2. **Colour**
3. **Hardness**

According to the TYPE they are

1. **Triticum Aestivum (also called hard wheat)**
2. **Triticum Compectum (also called soft wheat)**
3. **Triticum Durum (also called durum wheat)**

The Triticum Aestivum wheat flour contains more proteins. This flour is used for the production of bread.

The Triticum Compectum wheat flour contains low protein. So this flour is used for the production of biscuits, cakes and pastries.

The Triticum Durum wheat is mainly used to prepare semolina and macaroni.

According to the COLOUR they are

1. **Red wheat**
2. **White Wheat**

According to the HARDNESS they are

1. **Hard wheat**
2. **Soft Wheat**

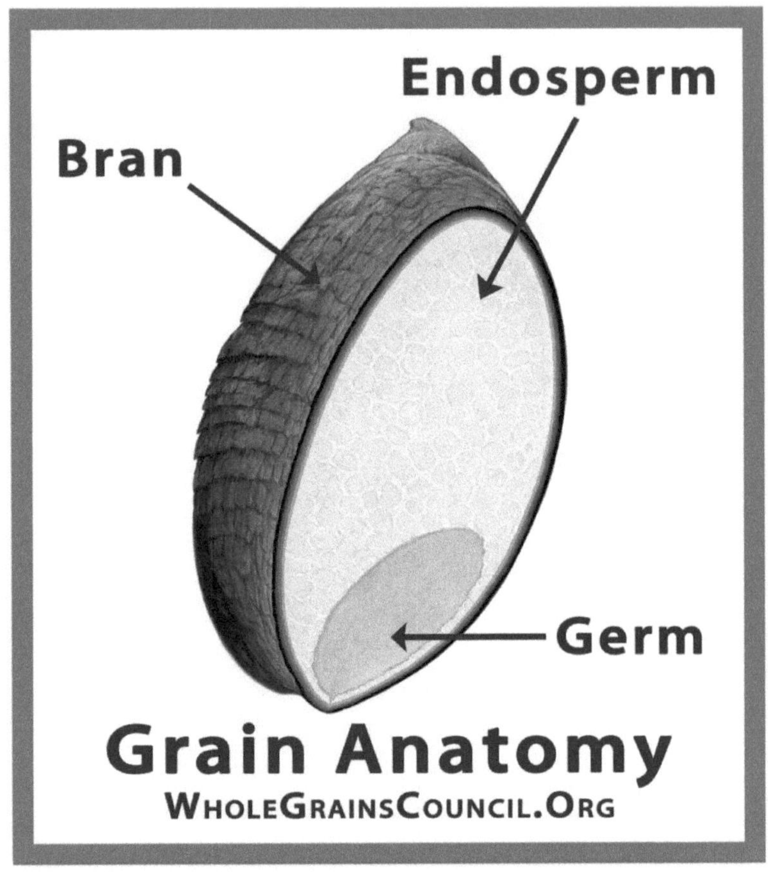

Wheat Anatomy

HARD WHEAT

Bakery products are made from this type of wheat flour, because had wheat flour contains the following characteristics.

1. **More protein**
2. **More Water Absorption Power (WAP)**
3. **Good mixing capacity that is easy to mix**

4. **Fermentation tolerance**
5. **Good gas retention power.**

SOFT WHEAT

Soft wheat flour contains the following characteristics

1. **Less Protein**
2. **Less Water Absorption Power**
3. **Poor mixing capacity**
4. **Poor fermentation tolerance**

The kernel of wheat is a storehouse of nutrients. The wheat is classified into 3 principal parts. They are

1. **Bran**
2. **Germ**
3. **Endosperm**

BRAN

Wheat contains 15% of bran. It is the outer portion of the Wheat. It has several layers. The colour of wheat is due to the testa. This layer protects the endosperm. The aleurone layer has small cells. These cells have enzymes, which converts starch into sugar and it gives softness to the flour.

Bran contains more nutritional value, even though it is removed during the milling process, as the sharp edges may cut down the gluten. Hence, the gas retention power is reduced and this in turn will reduce the volume of the bread.

During milling bran is removed and is used as animal feed.

GERM

Wheat contains 2.5% of germ. It is the sprouting section of the seed. During milling germ is removed because it has fat content that will spoil the flour quickly.

ENDOSPERM

Wheat contains 82.5% of endosperm. Although primarily starch it contains nutrients. During milling endosperm is separated from bran and germ.

TYPES OF FLOUR:

HIGH RATIO FLOUR:

This flour is also known as special cake flour. This type of flour absorbs high liquids, fats and sugar than normal flour. It is normally manufactured for special order and it is used in special recipes. This flour is normally bleached with chlorine gas.

WHOLE WHEAT FLOUR:

It is milled form whole wheat grain and no bran or germ is removed during milling. When using this flour, it requires more liquids than mentioned in the recipes.

WHOLE MEAL FLOUR (BROWN FLOUR)

In this mixture of refined flour, the content of bran and wheat germ are more. It can also be made by combining white and whole wheat flour.

SELF RAISING FLOUR:

It contains a certain quantity of baking powder. If we use this flour we should reduce the baking powder quantity.

Hard flour

The hardness and softness of the flour is determined how the endosperm is broken during the milling process.

This type of flour is used in the preparation of breakfast roles. This type of flour is obtained tends to be coarse.

Soft Flour

This type of flour will have a fine texture and the endosperm of the flour is milled to a final state. This type of flour is used for preparing cakes.

Strong Flour

It refers to the strength of the flour and its baking quality, strong flour produces large loaf volume, good crumb texture, and good keeping qualities it has high protein content, and this flour is generally used for making bread. This flour has a gluten content of 10 – 11.5 %. They can absorb more water than the weaker flour,

gluten proteins absorb about twice their won weight of water. They are also used for products which will have a high rise such as yeast goods, choux an also puff pastier. Strong flour is also known as Bakers flour.

Weak Flour

It has a less protein content, and forms only small loafs with coarse crumb structure this flour is suitable for cakes and biscuits. It has 7.85% of gluten and is also known as cake flour.

Medium flour

It is semi hard and used in the preparation of puries and chapattis.

ROLE OF FLOUR IN BAKERY PRODUCTS:

1. **It acts as the binding agents and an absorbing agent.**
2. **It is important for the flavour of products.**
3. **It adds the nutritional value to the product.**
4. **It builds the structure to the product.**
5. **It holds the other ingredients together and they are distributed evenly into the dough or mixture.**
6. **It is the back bone of the baked product.**
7. **It affects the shelf quality of products.**

SUGAR

Types of Sugar

Sugar is one of the major ingredients in the bakery industry and plays a vital role. Commonly sugar is obtained from sugar cane and beets. Sugars vary in their sweetening quality. There are different types of sugar. They are:

1. Granulated sugar 7.Treacle

2. Glucose or Invert syrup 8.Icing Sugar

3. Castor sugar 9.Honey

4. Sugar cubes 10.Jaggery

5. Nib Sugar 11.Loaf Sugar

6. Brown sugar 12.Golden syrup

Granulated Sugar

It is an all purpose crystal sugar and has large sized granuals, which is used in biscuits to get hard and crunchy texture. It is considered unsuitable for creaming mixture by manual process and ideal for boiled sugar works.

Icing sugar

Granulated sugar is ground and sieved through a fine mesh to produce a fine white powdered sugar. It contains calcium phosphate or starch to retain its free flowing capacity. It is mainly used for decorative purposes and is also called pulverized sugar.

Castor Sugar

It is a finely ground white crystallized sugar. It dissolves quickly and easily mixes with other ingredients. It gives a smooth structure to aerated products like cakes, sponges, short breads and shot pastries. It is also called confectionery sugar or powdered sugar.

Sugar Cubes

It is moulded form of powdered sugar. It is mainly used for beverages.

Loaf Sugar

It is a large compressed block of granulated sugar, which is cut into cubes. It does not dissolve easily. It is mainly used of boiled sugar work because of its purity.

Brown Sugar

It is unrefined sugar, which is in brown colour. There are 2 types. They are

1. Demerara Sugar
2. Barbados Sugar

Demerara Sugar

It is partially refined, fairly dry sugar, which is light brown in colour.This pale-coloured and mild-tasting raw cane *sugar* is named after its place of origin – *Demerara*, in Guyana

Barbados sugar

It is less refined, smaller grained moist sugar, which is dark brown in colour.

Demerara and Barbados sugars give dark colour and delicious flavour to the brown coloured cakes, biscuits and puddings. These sugars are also very popular and served with coffee.

Treacle

Treacle is any uncrystallized syrup made during the refining of sugar. Treacle is used both in cooking as a sweetener and as a condiment.. It is dark colour syrup with thick consistency. It is a slightly burnt sugar, which is mainly used for rich fruitcakes, puddings and biscuits.

Glucose or Invert syrup

I*nvert* sugar *syrup* is a mixture of *glucose* and fructose; it is obtained by splitting sucrose into these two components.. It is produced from starch or sucrose with the addition of weak acid to invert the sugar. It is available in thin syrup and in powdered form. It gives shining effect to fondant, it prevents crystallization in sugar boiling, it gives shelf life, retains the moisture for longer period in cakes and it can be used in chocolate to make it pliable.

Honey

Honey

It is a natural product extracted form the nectar of flowers by the honey bee. It gives delicious flavour and is used for making cakes, biscuits, brandy snaps and nought.

Jaggery

It is made from the extract of palm tree, which can be substitute for brown sugar.

Nib Sugar

Nib sugar (also pearl sugar and hail sugar) is a product of refined white sugar. The sugar is very coarse, hard, opaque white, and does not melt at temperatures typically used for baking.. It is broken sugar, which has been sieved to standardize the grain texture. It is mainly used for decorating the tops of cakes and buns.

Golden Syrup

Golden syrup is a pale treacle. It is a thick, amber-coloured form of inverted sugar syrup, made in the process of refining sugar cane or sugar beet juice into sugar, or by treatment of a sugar solution with acid. It is used in a variety of baking recipes and

desserts. It has an appearance similar to honey, and is often used as a substitute for honey by people who do not eat honey.

It is golden in colour and heavy in nature. It is a by product of sugar, refined after the boiling syrup ceases to yield crystals. It is filtered and concentrated and is used for ginger cakes, biscuits, tartlets, flans, steamed and baked puddings and sauces.

FUNCTION OF SUGAR IN BAKERY PRODUCTS

1. **Sugar is used as sweetener.**
2. **It acts as an energy food for yeast activity.**
3. **It produces co2 that raises the dough fabric (structure).**
4. **It improves the flavour and taste.**
5. **It retains moisture for a longer time and improves the shelf life.**
6. **Sugar caramelizes when heated which provides dark brown colour.**
7. **It gives smooth, soft, white texture grain and crumb.**
8. **It has a mellowing or tenderizing capacity.**
9. **It helps to give crust colour.**
10. **It gives nutritional value.**
11. **It improves the toasting quality.**
12. **In the form of icing sugar it is used for decorating purposes.**
13. **Sugar helps to get even texture.**
14. **When whisking egg whites, it gives the proteins an increased strength enabling them to retain a higher proportion of air.**
15. **Sugar lowers the freezing point in ice creams, keeping the mixture soft, smooth and free from ice grains.**

FATS AND OILS

Oil

Fats and oils appear as creams or fluid substances. The main difference between them is the melting point. When fat is heated it will melt and remain fairly firm at room temperature and become quite hard when chilled.

Oils are fluid at room temperature. When the oil is heated, it will change very little and becomes slightly thicker and cloudy in cold temperature.

For cake making, the emulsifying ability of the fat is important. The fat should be plastic in nature. There are different kinds of fat. Each fat has its own characteristics. So the quality of the fat is to be selected on the basis of the product, so that we get a quality end product.

Fats can be divided into two categories. They are

1. **Milk and Animal fat.**
2. **Vegetable fat compounds**

MILK AND ANIMAL FAT

1. **Butter**
2. **Lard**
3. **Suet**

Butter

Butter contains 82% of fat, 14% of water, 2% of protein and 2% of Minerals. The butter should be white in colour. The manufacturer adds colour for appearance. It should have a smooth firm, plastic texture, without trace of grain or oiliness. Butter has excellent creaming quality and when used for this purpose it should be soft but not oily. Butter has low melting points. So it is good for preparing puff pastry. It is available in slated and unsalted varieties. The unsalted butter is used for butter creams. If it is not stored properly the butter will get rancid.

Lard

It is a Pork fat and is a white solid fat. The fat content is 99%. It provides low flavour to the products. It is neutral in colour. It does not cream with sugar. It has a shortening power. It has less creaming quality. It is good for making lardly cake, flaky pastry and shallow frying.

Suet

It is found mostly around the kidney of beef or lamb. It is a hard white fat. The fat should be fresh, firm and dry with no unpleasant smell. To prepare suet, break down fat into small pieces and remove all skin and blood spots. Chop with a knife or grate with a fine grater. Keep the fat coated with some flour to prevent from sticking. This must be used cold and care must be taken when mixing with other ingredients. It is available in shredded or solid form. It is used for suet pastry, pudding and stuffing.

Suet has a melting point of between 45°C and 50°C (113°F and 122°F) and congelation between 37°C and 40°C. (98.6°F and 104°F). Its high smoke point makes it ideal for deep frying and pastry production.

VEGETABLE FAT COMPOUNDS

Palm Oil

1. **Margarine**
2. **White fat / Compound fat**
3. **Pastry fat**
4. **Special cake fat**

Margarine

Margarine is the substitute for butter. It is made from hydrogenous of vegetable oil. It contains 85% of fat. It has the ability to retain air during creaming operation. It lacks the flavour of butter. It is used only for bakery purposes. It may be salted and unsalted and has higher melting point.

White fat / Compound fat

It is 100% fat. It is white in colour. It is a substitute for lard. It has good shortening power and creaming quality. It can be used of

frying purposes and has a longer storage life than lard.

Pastry Fat

It is 100% fat. This is the toughest fat, which is white in colour. It has high melting point and instead of butter it can be used for puff pastry. It has the ability to be rolled and manipulated to produce the build up of layers in puff pastry. This special fat gives extra lift to the layers. Less fat is required to get the same effect.

Special cake fat

These are high ratio fat and have high grade shortening power. They have the ability to hold high proportion of sugar and liquids and should be used with special flour to produce very light cakes and sponges. Special recipes and methods of production are required when using this fat.

OILS

Edible Oil

Edible oils are derived form fruits seeds and nuts. These oils have a limited purpose in pastry work, as they do not have the

ability to hold air. They are used mainly in mixtures where shortening and aeration are not essential. They are mainly used for deep and shallow frying and also for greasing of trays and moulds.

FUNCTIONS OF FAT IN BAKERY PRODUCTS

1. **Fat provides nutrition and flavour.**
2. **It makes the product tender and palatable**
3. **It helps to retain air during creaming operation; it increases volume to the produces.**
4. **It gives softness to the product.**
5. **It improves the taste and shelf life of the products.**
6. **It gives good flavour and colour.**
7. **In bread dough it provides extensibility**
8. **In bread it improves the texture and grain**
9. **In biscuit it is used for shortening value.**
10. **It increases eating quality of the products.**

EGGS

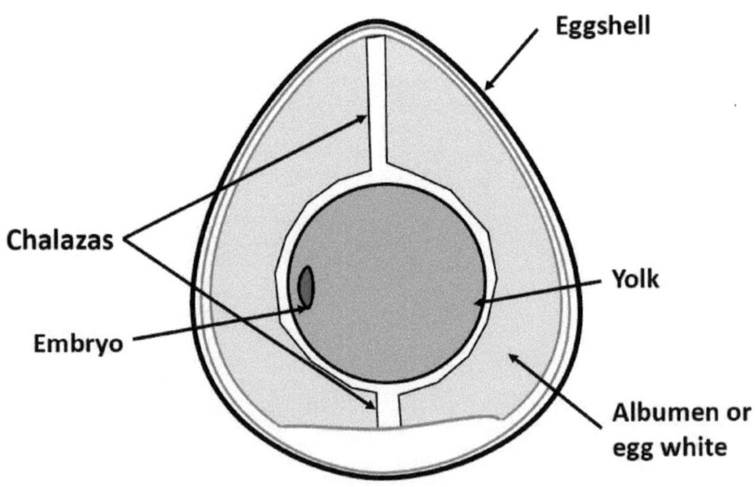

Parts of Egg

Eggs are most important raw material for different bakery products. Eggs are used in most of the bakery products. Ducks, geese and turkeys eggs can also be used for production. As these eggs have different characteristics bakers prefers hen eggs only.

COMPOSITION OF EGGS

Eggs are composed of three parts. They are

1. Shell - 12%

2. White / Albumen - 58%

3. Yolk - 30%

There are different grades and sizes of eggs available in the market. The average egg weight starts form 45gms to 70gms.

TYPES OF EGGS

There are two eggs used in bakeries. They are

1. **Shelled eggs**
2. **Frozen eggs.**

Shelled Eggs

Quality eggs must be used to ensure quality in the finished products.

Frozen Eggs

Frozen Eggs have the following advantages

1. **They save time and labour because breaking and separating are not necessary**
2. **They avoid waste through spoilage and other causes.**
3. **An adequate supply of uniform quality is assured and uniform quality means better results.**

Frozen eggs are solid as whole eggs, yolks, white or specials, which contains whole eggs and extra yolks.

FUNCTIONS OF EGG IN BAKERY PRODUCTS

1. **It provides structure to the products**
2. **It provides moisture to the products.**
3. **It gives flavour.**
4. **It improves the product taste.**
5. **It gives nutritional value.**
6. **Lecithin present in the egg yolk acts as an emulsifier.**
7. **Lutin also found in yolk imports colour.**
8. **During beating small air cell are incorporated and increase the volume of the products**
9. **Egg improves the grain and texture quality.**
10. **It gives softness to the products.**
11. **It is used as a thickening agent as well as binding agent**
12. **Egg yolk contains fat is has a shortening action.**
13. **Egg wash gives a shining appearance to pastry and baked dough products.**

YEAST

Yeast

Next to flour, yeast is the most important ingredient for yeast products. It is a living microorganism and is a form of plant life, which cannot be seen by naked eyes. Yeast was discovered by Louis

Pasteur in the year 1859.

Structure of Yeast

Size and Shape

The diameter of yeas is 1/2500 inch. Yeast appears round the oval.

FUNCTIONS OF YEAST IN BAKERY PRODUCTS

1. **When yeast is mixed with flour into dough, it releases co2 it helps to raise the dough.**
2. **Yeast increases the volume, improves the grain, the texture and flavor to the baked products**
3. **For conditioning the dough so that is attains sufficient mellowness to stretch under the pressure of co2 gas and form structure of the products.**

SALT

Enter Caption

The chemical name of salt is sodium chloride and formula is NACL. It is composed of 40% of sodium and 60% of chlorine. It is white crystalline product. It should completely dissolve in water and should not have any foreign particles. Salt is used in the bakery for many reasons for salt enhances the natural flavour of other ingredients.

Salt has a distinctive taste, transforms an insipid dish to a wonderful dish. It should be used skillfully for too much of it could spoil the product.

FUNCTIONS OF SALT IN BAKERY PRODUCTS

1. **It helps to control the yeast activity in bakery products.**
2. **It improves the flavour of the products.**
3. **The crust colour of the product is improved by lowering the caramelization temperature of the sugar.**
4. **It enhances the natural flavour of other ingredients.**
5. **Certain cakes have more sugar in the formula so salt helps to cut down the excessive sweetness.**
6. **Salt helps to keep bakery products fresh and deeps it moist for a longer time.**
7. **Salt has a tightening action on flour proteins. It improves the gas retention power of the dough.**
8. **It improves the texture and grain of baked products.**
9. **Salt helps to prevent the formation and growth of undesirable bacteria at a certain level in the yeast raised dough.**
10. **The amount of slat to be used depends upon the type of lour which we use weak flour will take more slat and also a rich formula salt gives strengthen effect to the purpose. The quantity of salt will generally vary from 1.5 to 2%**
11. **it improves the WAP**
12. **It controls the production of unwanted acids in dough.**

II

Yeast Dough

All yeast dough are made according to the same basic principles, it is useful to divide yeast product into categories such as the following.

Yeast

Lean Dough Products:
Lean dough is one that is low in fat and sugar.

- **Hard-crusted breads and rolls, including French and Italian breads, Kaiser Rolls and other hard rolls, and pizza. These are the leanest of all bread products.**
- **Other white and whole wheat breads and dinner rolls. These have a higher fat and sugar content and sometime also contain eggs and milk solids. Because they are slightly richer, they generally have soft crusts.Bread made with other grains. Rye breads are the most common. Many varieties of rye bread are produced, with light or dark flours.**

Rich Dough Products:

- **Non sweet breads and rolls, including rich dinner rolls and brioche. They have a high fat content but their sugar content is low enough to allow them to be served as dinner breads. Brioche dough, made with a high proportion of butter and eggs, is especially rich.**

- **Sweet rolls including coffee cakes and many breakfast and tea rolls. This has high fat and sugar content and usually contains eggs. They generally have sweet filling or topping.**

Laminated or Rolled – In yeast dough products: Rolled-in yeast dough or laminated dough are those in which a fat is incorporated into the dough in many layers by using a rolling and folding procedure. The alternating layers of fat and dough give the baked product a flaky texture.

Laminated dough vary in sugar content from about 4% for some croissant dough to 15% or more for some Danish dough. However, most of the sweetness of laminated yeast dough products comes from the filling and toppings.

Croissant and Danish dough are the main laminated yeast dough product. In general, Danish dough products contain eggs, while croissants does not.

Yeast Dough Production:

There are twelve basic steps in the production of yeast breads. These steps are generally applied to all yeast products, with variations depending on the particular product.

They are

1. Scaling ingredients 7. Benching

2. Mixing 8. Makeup and Panning

3. Bulk Fermentation 9. Proofing

4. Folding or Punching 10. Baking

5. Scaling or Portioning of dough 11. Cooling

6. Rounding 12. Storing

Scaling Ingredients:

Scaling

All ingredients must be weighted accurately.

Water, milk and eggs may be measured by volume. They are scaled at 1 Pint per Pound (1 kg/L). However, it is more accurate to weight these liquids, especially if quantities are large.

Special care must be taken when measuring spices and other ingredients used in very small quantities. This is particularly

important with salt, which affects the rate of fermentation.

Mixing:

Mixing

Mixing yeast dough has three main purposes

1. To combine all ingredients into a uniform, smooth dough.

2. To distribute the yeast evenly throughout the dough.

3. To develop the gluten.

Bulk Fermentation:

Fermentation is a process by which yeast acts on the sugars and starches in the dough to produce carbon dioxide gas (CO_2) and alcohol. Gluten becomes smoother and more elastic during fermentation, so it stretches farther and holds more gas. An under fermentation dough will not develop proper volume and the texture of the product will be coarse.A dough that ferments too long or at too high temperature becomes sticky, hard to work and slightly sour. An under fermented dough is called as young dough. An over fermented dough is called as old dough.Yeast action

continues until the yeast cells are killed when the temperature of the dough reaches 140'F in the oven.

Folding Or Punching:

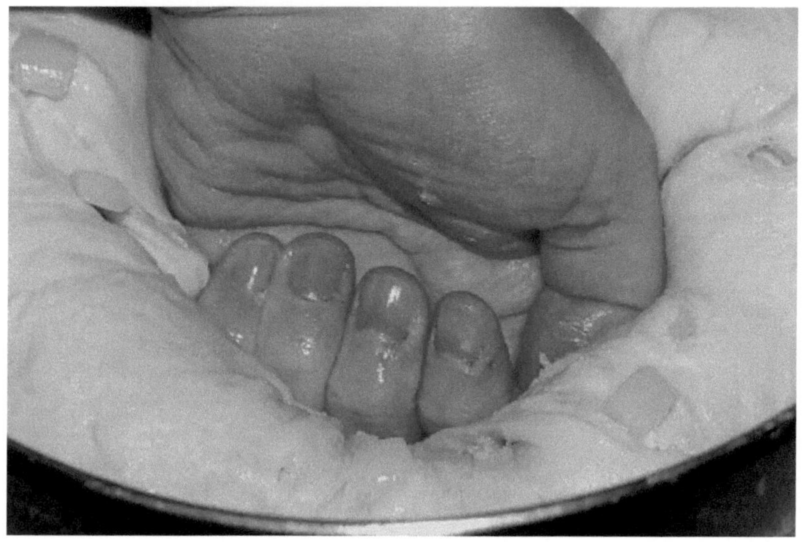

Punching

After fermentation is completed, the dough is folded over to compress it and to give additional slight development to the gluten. This step accomplishes four objectives:

1. It expels carbon dioxide.

2. It redistributes the yeast for further growth.

3. It relaxes the gluten.

4. It equalizes the temperature throughout the dough.

Folding the dough after bulk fermentation is traditionally called punching. For some products additional bulk fermentation and folding may be required after this step, although most bread need only one bulk fermentation period.

Large quantities of dough are more easily folded on a workbench, although small batches can easily be folded in the bowl or container in which they are fermented.

Scaling or Portioning Dough

Scaling or Portioning Dough

Using a baker's scale, divide the dough into pieces of the same weight, according to the product being made.

During scaling, allowance is made for weight loss due to evaporation of moisture in the oven. This weight loss is approximately 10 to 13% of the weight of the dough. Allow an extra 11/2 to 2 ounces dough for each 1 pound baked bread, or 50 to 65 g per 500 g.

Actual baking loss depends on baking time, size of the unit, and whether it is baked in a pan or freestanding.

Scaling should be done rapidly and efficiently to avoid over fermenting the dough.

ROUNDING

Rolling

After scaling, the pieces of dough are shaped into smooth, round balls. This procedure forms a kind of skin by stretching the gluten on the outside of the dough into a smooth layer. Rounding simplifies the later shaping of the dough and also helps retain gases produced by the yeast.

Machines are also available that divide and round portions of dough automatically.

Benching, bench Proofing, or Intermediate Proofing

Rounded portions of dough are allowed to rest for 10 to 20 minutes. This is relaxes the gluten to make shaping the dough easier. Also fermentation continues during this time.

In large operations, the rounded dough is placed in special proofers for this rest. Smaller operations place the dough in boxes that are stacked on one another to keep the dough covered. Or the dough may simply be placed on the workbench and covered - hence the term benching or bench rest.

MAKEUP AND PANNING

The sought is shaped into loaves or rolls and then placed in pans or on baking sheets. Hearth breads – breads baked directly on the bottom of the oven may be placed in floured baskets or other molds after makeup.

Proper makeup or molding is of critical importance to the finished baked product. All gas bubbles should be expelled during molding. Bubbles left in the dough will result in large air holes in the baked product.

For both pan breads and hearth breads, the seam must be centered on the bottom to avoid splitting during baking. For units baked in pans, the pan size must be matched to the weight of the dough. Too little or too much dough will result in a poorly shaped loaf. Breads and rolls take a great many forms. Many shapes and techniques are presented.

ROOFING

Proofing is a continuation of the process of yeast fermentation that increases the volume of the shaped dough. Bakers use two terms so they can distinguish between fermentation of the mixed dough and proofing of the made up product before baking. Proofing temperatures are generally higher than fermentation temperature.

Under proofing results in poor volume and dense texture. Overproofing results in coarse texture and some loss of flavor. French bread is generally given a long proof to create its characteristic open texture. Its strong gluten withstands the extra stretching of a long proof.

Rich dough are slightly under proofed because their weaker gluten structure does not withstand too much stretching.

BAKING

Many changes take place in the dough during baking.

1. **Over spring, which is the rapid rising in the oven due to production and expansion trapped gases as a result of the oven**

heat. The yeast is very active at first but is killed when the temperature inside the dough reaches 140oF (60oC).

2. **Coagulation of proteins and gelatinization of starches. In other words, the product becomes firm and holds its shape.**

3. Formation and browning of the crust.

In order to control the baking process, the following factors should be considered.

OVEN TEMPERATURE AND BAKING TIME

Temperatures must be adjusted for the product being baked. At the proper temperature, the inside of the unit becomes completely baked at the same time the crust achieves the desired color.

Therefore:

1. **Large units are baked at a lower temperature and for a longer time than small rolls spaced apart.**

2. **Rich dough and sweet dough are baked at a lower temperature because their fat, sugar, and milk content makes them brown faster.**

3 . French breads made with no added sugar and a long fermentation requires very high temperatures to achieve the desired crust color.

Popular American lean breaks are baked at 400o to 425oF

Some French bread are baked at 425o to 475o

Rich products are baked at 350o to 400o F

A golden brown crust color is the normal indication of doneness. Loaves that are done sound hollow when thumped.

WASHES

Many, if not most, yeast products are brushed with a liquid, called a wash, just before baking. The most common washes are as follows.

1. Water is used primarily for hard – crusted products, such as French bread. Like Stream in the oven, the water helps keep the crust from drying too quickly and thus becoming to thick.

2. Starch paste is used primarily for rye breads. In addition to keeping the crust from drying too quickly, the starch paste helps give a shine to the crust. To make a starch paste, mix 1 ounce light rye flour with 1 quart water. Bring to a boil while stirring. Cool. If necessary, thin with water to the consistency of cream.

3. Egg wash is used to give a shiny brown crust to soft breads and rolls and to rich dough and Danish. It is made by mixing beaten eggs with water or, sometimes, milk. Proportions vary greatly depending on how strong a wash is desired.

4. Commercial aerosol washes provide a quick and easy way to give shine and also to help toppings such as seeds adhere.

CUTTING OR SCORING

A break on the side of the loaf is caused by continued rising after the crust is formed. To allow for this expansion, the tops of hard – crusted breads are cut before baking. Slashes are made on the top of the loaf with a baker's lame or other sharp knife or razor immediately before it is put into the oven, as shown in the figure. The pattern created by the cuts also contributes to the appearance of the bread.

Small rolls often bake completely without a break, so they are usually cut for the sake of appearance only.

Note: The term docking is often used for this procedure. However, many bakers feel this term should be reserved for a different process – namely, the piercing or perforating of pastry

and pie dough.

LOADING THE OVENS

Proofed dough are fragile until they become set by baking. They should be handled carefully when being loaded into the ovens, and they should not be disturbed during the first part of baking.

Breads and rolls are baked either directly on the bottom of the oven or in pans.

1. **Hearth Breads. To load the ovens, place the proofed units on a peel that is well dusted with cornmeal. Slide the peel into the oven. Then, with a quick snap, remove the peel, leaving the loaves or rolls in place. To remove baked items, quickly slide the peel under them and pull them out.**
2. **Pan Breads and rolls. Freestanding items may be baked on sheet pans instead of on the hearth. Bakers generally refer to such breads and rolls as hearth breads even if they are not baked directly on the bottom of the oven. Sprinkle the pans with cornmeal to keep the units form sticking and to stimulate the appearance of hearth – baked items. Pans may also be lined with silicone paper. Perforated sheet pans or screens are also available. These allow better air circulation and therefore permit more even browning.**

STEAM

Hard – crusted breads are baked with stream injected into the ovens during the first part of the baking period. Rye breads are benefit from baking with steam for the first 10 minutes.

The Steam helps keep the crust soft during the first part of baking so the bread can expand rapidly and evenly without cracking or breaking. If steam were not used, the crust would begin forming earlier and thus would become thick and heavy. Also, crust that forms too easily is likely to split as the interior

continues to expand. The steam also helps distribute the heat in the oven, further aiding oven spring. When the moisture of the steam reacts with the starches on the surface, some of the starches form dextrins. Then, when the steam is withdrawn, these dextrins, along with sugars in the dough, caramelize and turn brown. The result is a thin, crisp, glazed crust.

Rich Dough, those with higher fat or sugar content, does not form crisp crusts and are usually baked without stream.

COOLING

After baking, bread must be removed form the pans and cooled on racks to allow the escape of the excess moisture and alcohol created during fermentation.

Small rolls spaced on baking sheets are often cooled on the pans when air circulation is adequate. On the other hand, if condensation is likely to make the bottoms of the rolls soggy, it is better to cool them on racks.

If soft crusts are desired, bread in a draft because the crust may crack.

Like other dough products, breads continue to undergo physical and chemical changes after they are removed from the oven.

STORING

Breads to be served within 8 hours may be left on racks. For longer storage, wrap cooled breads in moisture proof bags to retard staling. Breads must be thoroughly cool before wrapping, or moisture will collect inside the bags.

Wrapping and freezing maintains quality for longer periods. Refrigeration, on the other hand, increases staling.

Hard – crusted breads should not be wrapped because the crusts will soften and become leathery. Alternatively, use porous bags or wrapping material that protects the bread form

contamination but allows moisture to escape.

TYPES OF DOUGH – MAKING PROCESSES

The dough is then given a bulk fermentation time of 1 to 2 ½ Hours. This is called a short – fermentation straight dough.

A no-time dough is made with a large quantity of yeast, preferably instant dry yeast, taken form the mixer at a higher temperature and given only a few minutes rest before being scaled and made up. It is also given a shorter proof. This process should be used only in emergencies because the final product does not have a good texture and flavor.

Long – fermentation dough are fermented for 5 to 6 hours or longer, sometimes overnight, at a temperature of 75o F or lower. During this time, it is usually advisable to fold or punch the dough several times. The advantage of this method is that the long, slow fermentation greatly enhances the flavor of the product. Some of the best European breads are made this way. The major disadvantages – besides being harder on the work schedule – are that the fermentation is harder to control because of fluctuation in temperature and other factors. Dough often become over fermented. In spite of this disadvantage, long fermentation has been revived with the interest in artisan breads.

SPONGE PROCESSES

The sponge process involves a two – stage mixing method. First, a sponge is made of water, flour, and yeast and allowed to ferment then the dough is made by mixing in the remaining ingredients. The finished dough may be given a short fermentation, or, if the sponge has had long fermentation, it may be scaled immediately, like a no – time dough.

ADVANTAGES OF THE SPONGE METHOD

Shorter fermentation time for the finished dough.

Scheduling flexibility. Sponges can usually be held longer than finished dough. Increased flavor, developed by the long fermentation of the sponge. Stronger fermentation of rich dough. High sugar and fat content inhibits yeast growth. When the sponge method is used, most of the fermentation is complete before the fat and sugar are incorporated.

Less yeast is needed, because it multiplies during the sponge fermentation.

CONTROLLING FERMENTATION

Proper fermentation – that is, fermentation that produces dough that is neither under ripe nor overripe – requires a balance of time, temperature, and yeast quantity.

TIME

Fermentation times vary, so that time to punch the dough is indicated not by clock but by the appearance and feel of the dough. To vary the fermentation time, you must control the dough temperature and the amount of yeast.

TEMPERATURE

Ideally, dough is fermented at the temperature at which it is taken form the mixer. Large bakeries have special fermentation rooms for controlling temperature and humidity, but small bakeshops and restaurant kitchens seldom have this luxury. If a short – fermentation process is used, however the fermentation is complete before the dough is greatly affected by changes in shop temperature.

WATER TEMPERATURE

Dough must be at the proper temperature, usually 78o to 80oF, in order to ferment at the desired rate. The temperature of the dough is affected by several factors:

1. Shop temperature

2. Flour Temperature

3. Water Temperature

Of these, water temperature is the easiest to control in the small bakeshop. Therefore, when the water is scaled, it should be brought to the required temperature. On cold days, it may have to be warmed, and on hot days, using a mixture of crushed ice and water may be necessary. Also, if a long fermentation is used, the dough temperature must be reduced in order to avoid over fermenting.

BREAD FAULTS AND THEIR CAUSES

FAULT	CAUSES
SHAPE	
Poor Volume	Too much salt Too little yeast Too little liquid Weak flour Under or over mixing Oven too hot
Too Much Volume	Too little salt Too much yeast Too much dough scaled Over proofed
Poor Shape	Too much liquid Flour too weak Improper molding or makeup Improper fermentation or proofing Too much oven steam
Split or Burst crust	Over mixing Under fermented dough Improper molding – seam not on bottom Uneven heat in oven Oven too hot Insufficient steam

shape -FAULT

FLAVOR	
Flat taste	Too little salt
Poor flavor	Inferior, spoiled, or rancid ingredients Poor bakeshop sanitation Under or over fermented
Texture and Crumb	
Too dense or close– grained	Too much salt Too little liquid Too little yeast Under fermented Under proofed
Too coarse or Open	Too much yeast Too much liquid Incorrect mixing time Improper fermentation Over proofed Pan too large
Streaked crumb	Improper mixing procedure Poor molding or makeup techniques Too much flour used for dusting
Poor texture or crumbly	Flour too weak Too little salt Fermentation time too long or too short Over proofed Baking temperature too low
Gray crumb	Fermentation time or temperature too high

FLAVOR - FAULT

Crust	
Too dark	Too much sugar or milk Under fermented dough Oven temperature too high Baking time too long Insufficient stream at beginning of baking
Too pale	Too little sugar or milk Over fermented dough Over proofed Oven temperature to low Baking time too short Too much steam in oven
Too Thick	Too little sugar or fat Improper fermentation Baked too long or at wrong temperature Too little steam
Blisters on crust	Too much liquid Improper fermentation Improper shaping of loaf.

CRUST -FAULT

III

Biscuits-Meaning and Preparation

Biscuits-meaning and preparation

Cookies- Production, Sandwich Cookies, Ice box Cookies, bar Cookies, macaroons, wafers and lace cookies, assorted cookies

Biscuit

A **biscuit** is a Baked dible, and commonly flour-based food-product.

Confectionery biscuits

Early biscuits were hard, dry, and unsweetened. They were most often cooked after bread, in a cooling bakers' oven; they were a cheap form of sustenance for the poor.

By the seventh century AD, cooks of the Persian empire had learnt from their forebears the secrets of lightening and enriching bread-based mixtures with eggs, butter, and cream, and sweetening them with fruit and honey. One of the earliest spiced biscuits was gingerbread, meaning "spice bread", brought to Europe by the Armenian monk Grégoire de Nicopolis. This was originally a dense, treaclely (molasses-based) spice cake or bread. As it was so expensive to make, early ginger biscuits were a cheap form of using up the leftover bread mix.

As the making and quality of bread had been controlled to this point, so were the skills of biscuit making through the Craft Guilds. As the supply of sugar began, and the refinement and supply of flour increased, so did the ability to sample more leisurely foodstuffs, including sweet biscuits. The first documented trade of gingerbread biscuits dates to the 16th century, where they were sold in monastery pharmacies and town square farmers markets. Gingerbread became widely available in the 18th century. Hence it is no surprise that, often together with local farm produce of meat and cheese, many regions of the world have their own distinct style of biscuit, and so old is this form of food.

Biscuits today

Most modern biscuits can trace their origins back to either the hardtack ship's biscuit, or the creative art of the baker:

- Ship's biscuit derived: Digestive, rich tea, Abernethy, cracker
- Baker's art: Biscuit rose de Reims

Biscuits today can be savoury or sweet, but most are small at around 2 inches (5.1 cm) in diameter, and flat. The term biscuit also applies to sandwich-type biscuits, wherein a layer of cream or icing is sandwiched between two biscuits, such as the custard cream, or a layer of jam (as in biscuits which, in the United Kingdom, are known as "Jammy Dodgers")uits are commonly eaten as a snack food, and are, in general, made with wheat flour or oats, and sweetened with sugar or honey. Varieties may contain chocolate, fruit, jam, nuts, or even be used to sandwich other fillings. There is usually a dedicated section for sweet biscuits in most European supermarkets.In Britain, the digestive biscuit and rich tea have a strong cultural identity as the traditional accompaniment to a cup of tea, and are regularly eaten as such. Many tea drinkers "dunk" their biscuits in tea, allowing them to absorb liquid and soften slightly before consumption.y biscuits or crackers (such as cream crackers, water biscuits, oatcakes, or crisp breads) are usually plainer and commonly eaten with cheese following a meal. Also among the savoury biscuit we may include the Jewish biscuits known as Matzos. A large variety of savoury biscuits also contain additional ingredients for flavour or texture, such as poppy seeds, onion or onion seeds, cheese (such as cheese melts), and olives. Savoury biscuits also usually have a dedicated section in most European supermarkets, often in the same aisle as sweet biscuits. The exceto savoury biscuits is the sweetmeal digestive known as the "Hovis biscuit", which, although slightly sweet, is still classified as a cheese biscuit. Savoury biscuits sold in supermarkets are sometimes associated with a certain geographical area, such as Scottish oatcakes or Cornish wafer biscuits.In general, Australians, South Africans, New Zealanders, Kenyans, Indians, Pakistanis, Sri Lankans, Singaporeans, and the Irish use the British meaning of "biscuit" for the sweet biscuit. In both Canada and Australasia, the terms biscuit and cookie are used interchangeably, depending on the region and the speaker, with biscuits usually referring to hard, sweet biscuits (such as digestives, Nice, Bourbon creams, etc.) and cookies for soft baked goods (i.e. chocolate chip cookies). Two famous Australasian biscuit varieties are the ANZAC biscuit and the Tim Tam. This sense is at the root of the name of the United States' most prominent maker of cookies and crackers, the National Biscuit Company, now called Nabisco.

iscuits-Meaning and Preparation:

It may be defined as small cakes made from flour, sugar, fat, egg with flavor. It contains 50% of fat. It is thin and flat. It is dry and crispy. It has a crumble texture. It is prepared by the sheeting process.

BISCUIT MIXTURES

Biscuits may be produced by the following methods:

1. Rubbing in 4.Flour batter
2. Foaming 5.Blending
3. Sugar Batter

RUBBING IN

This is Probably the best known method and is used in producing some of the most famous types of biscuits, such as shortbread. The method is exactly the same as producing short pastry.

- Rub the fat into the flour, by hand or by machine, adding the liquid and the sugar and mixing in the flour to produce a smooth biscuit paste.
- Do not overwork the paste otherwise it will not combine and as a consequence you will not be able to roll it out.

FOAMING

This is where foam is produced from egg whites or egg yolks or both. Sponge fingers are an example of a two foam mixture. Meringue is an example of a single foam mixture using egg whites. Great care must be taken not to over mix the product.

SUGAR BATTER METHOD

Fat and Sugar are mixed together to produce a light and fluffy cream. Beaten egg is gradually added. The dry ingredients are then carefully folded in.

FLOUR BATTER METHOD

Half the sieved flour is creamed with the fat. The eggs and sugar are beaten together before they are added to the fat and flour mixture. Finally, the remainder of the flour is folded in together with any other dry ingredients.

BLENDING METHOD

In several biscuit recipes, the method only requires the chef to blend all the ingredients together to produce a smooth paste.

PRODUCTION METHODS AND EXAMPLES

- Rubbing in Shortbread.
- Foaming Sponge fingers.
- Sugar batter method Cats' tongues (using basic almond commercial mixture).

COOKIE

The word cookie means small cake, and that is exactly what a cookie is. In fact, some cookies are made from cake batter. For some products, such as certain kinds of brownies, it's difficult to know whether to classify them as cakes or cookies.

Most cookie formulas, however, call for less liquid than cake formulas do. Cookie doughs range from soft to very stiff, unlike the thinner batters for cakes. This difference in moisture content means

some differences in mixing methods, although the basic procedures are much like those for cakes.

The most apparent differences between cakes and cookies are in the makeup. Because most cookies are individually formed or shaped, a great deal of hand labor is involved. Learning correct methods and practicing diligently are essential for efficiency.

COOKIE CHARACTERISTICS AND THEIR CAUSES

Cookies come in an infinite variety of shapes, sizes, flavors, and textures. Characteristics that are desirable in some are not desirable in others. For example, we want some cookies to be crisp and others to be soft. We want some to hold their shape and others to spread during baking. In order to produce the characteristics we want and to correct faults, it is useful to know what causes these characteristics.

CRISPNESS

Cookies are crisp if they are very low in moisture. The following factors contribute to crispness:

portion of liquid in the mix. Most crisp cookies are made from stiff dough.

2. High sugar and fat content.

3. Evaporation of moisture during baking due to high temperatures and/or long baking.

4. Small size or thin shape, so the cookies dry quickly during baking.

5. Proper storage. Crisp cookies can become soft if they absorb moisture.

SOFTNESS

Softness is the opposite of crispness, so it has the opposite causes, as follows:

1. High proportion of liquid in mix.

2. Low sugar and fat.

3. Honey, molasses, or corn syrup included in formulas. These sugars are **hygroscopic**, which means they readily absorb moisture from the air or from their surroundings.

4. Underbaking.

5. Large size or thick shape. The cookies retain moisture.

6. Proper storage. Soft cookies can become stale and dry if not tightly covered or wrapped.

CHEWINESS

Moisture is necessary for chewiness, but other factors are also required. In other words, all chewy cookies are soft, but not all soft cookies are chewy.

1. High sugar and liquid content, but low fat content.

2. High proportion of eggs.

3. Strong flour, or gluten developed during mixing.

SPREAD

Spread is desirable in some cookies, while others must hold their shape. Several factors contribute to spread or lack of spread.

1. Sugar.

High sugar content increases spread. Coarse granulated sugar increases spread, whereas fine sugar or confectioners' sugar reduces spread.

2. Leavening.

High baking soda or baking ammonia content encourages spread. So does long creaming, which incorporates air.

3. Temperature.

Low oven temperature increases spread. High temperature decreases spread because the cookie sets up before it has a chance to spread too much.

4. Liquid.

A slack batter—that is, one with a high liquid content—spreads more than stiff dough.

5. Flour.

Strong flour or activation of gluten decreases spread.

6. Pan grease.

Cookies spread more if baked on a heavily greased pan.

MIXING METHODS

Cookie-mixing methods are much like cake-mixing methods. The major difference is that less liquid is usually incorporated, so mixing is somewhat easier. Less liquid means that gluten is less developed by the mixing. Also, a smooth, uniform mix is easier to obtain.

There are three basic cookie mixing methods:

1. One-stage

2. Creaming

3. Sponge

These methods are subject to many variations due to differences in formulas. The general procedures are as follows. Be sure, however, to follow the exact instructions when a formula indicates a variation in the procedure.

ONE-STAGE METHOD

The **one-stage method** is the counterpart of the blending or two-stage cake-mixing method, discussed in the previous chapter. Cake batters have more liquid, so it must be added in two or more stages in order to blend uniformly. Low-moisture cookies, on the other hand, can be mixed all in one stage.

CREAMING METHOD

The **creaming method** for cookies is nearly identical to the creaming method for cakes. Because cookies require less liquid, it is not necessary to add the liquid alternately with the flour. It can be added all at once.

SPONGE METHOD

The **sponge method** for cookies is essentially the same as the egg-foam methods for cakes. The procedure varies considerably, depending on the ingredients. Batches should be kept small because the batter is delicate.

TYPES AND MAKEUP METHODS

We can classify cookie types by makeup method as well as by mixing method. Grouping by the makeup method is perhaps more useful from the point of view of production because mixing methods are relatively simple, whereas makeup procedures vary considerably.

In this section, we present basic procedures for producing seven COOKIE TYPES:

1. Dropped

2. Bagged

3. Rolled

4. Molded

5. Icebox

6. Bar

7. Sheet

No matter what makeup method you use, follow one important rule: Make all cookies of uniform size and thickness. This is essential for even baking. Because baking times are so short, small cookies may burn before large ones are done.

DROPPED COOKIESDropped cookies

are made from soft dough or batter. They are fast and easy to make up. Many sponge or foam-type batters are made up as dropped cookies.

1. Select the proper size scoop for accurate portioning.

No.30 scoop makes a large cookie, about 1 oz (30 g).

No.40 scoop makes a medium cookie.

Nos.50, 60, or small scoops make small cookies.

2. Drop the cookies onto the prepared baking sheets. Allow enough space between cookies for spreading.

3. Rich cookies spread by themselves. However, if the formula requires it, flatten the mounds of batter slightly with a weight dipped in sugar.

BAGGED COOKIES

Bagged cookies, or pressed cookies, are also made from soft doughs. The dough must be soft enough to be forced through a pastry bag but stiff enough to hold its shape.

1. Fit a pastry bag with a tip of the desired size and shape. Fill the bag with the cookie dough.

2. Press out cookies of desired shape and size directly onto prepared cookie sheets.

ROLLED COOKIES

Rolled cookies, which are cut from stiff dough, are not often made in commercial food service because they require excessive labor. Also, scraps are always left over after cutting. When rerolled, these scraps make inferior, tough cookies.

1. Chill dough thoroughly.

2. Roll dough to **18** inch (3 mm) thick on a floured canvas or floured workbench. Use as little flour as possible for dusting because the flour can toughen the cookies.

3. Cut out cookies with cookie cutters and place on prepared baking sheets. Cut as close together as possible to reduce the quantity of scraps.

OLDED COOKIES

The first part of the procedure for **molded cookies** is simply a fast and fairly accurate way of dividing the dough into equal portions. Each piece is then molded into the desired shape. This usually consists of simply flattening the pieces out with a weight. For some traditional cookies, special molds are used to flatten the dough and, at the same time, stamp it with a design.

The pieces may also be shaped by hand into crescents, fingers, or other shapes.

1. Roll the dough into long cylinders about 1 inch (2.5 cm) thick, or whatever size is required.(Refrigerate the dough if it is too soft to handle.)

2. With a knife or bench scraper, cut the roll into 1-ounce (30-g) pieces, or whatever size is required.

3. Place the pieces on prepared baking sheets, leaving 2 inches (5 cm) of space between them.

4. Flatten cookies with a weight (such as a can) dipped in granulated sugar after pressing each cookie.

A fork is sometimes used for flattening the dough, as for peanut butter cookies.

5. Alternative method: After step 2, shape the dough by hand into desired shapes.

ICEBOX COOKIES

The **icebox method**, or *refrigerator method,* is ideal for operations that wish to have freshly baked cookies on hand at all times. The rolls of dough may be made up in advance and stored. Cookies can easily be cut and baked as needed.

1. Scale dough into pieces of uniform size, from 700 g, if you are making small cookies, to 1400 g, for large cookies.

2. Form the dough into cylinders from 1 to 2 inches (2.5 to 5 cm) in diameter, depending on the size cookie desired.

For accurate portioning, it is important to make all the cylinders of dough the same thickness and length.

3. Wrap the cylinders in parchment or waxed paper, place them on sheet pans, and refrigerate overnight.

4. Unwrap the dough and cut into slices of uniform thickness. The exact thickness required depends on the size of the cookie and how much the dough spreads during baking. The usual range is from (3 to 12 mm).

A slicing machine is recommended for ensuring even thickness. Doughs containing nuts or fruits should be sliced by hand with a knife.

1. Place the slices on prepared baking sheets, allowing 2 inches (5 cm) of space between cookies.

BAR COOKIES

Bar cookies are so called because the dough is shaped into long bars, which are baked and then cut. After cutting, they may be baked again, as in the case of biscotto, which means “twice baked.” Do not confuse bar cookies with sheet cookies , which are often called bars by consumers.

1. Scale the dough into (800-g) units (500-g units, may be used for smaller cookies).

2. Shape the pieces of dough into cylinders the length of the sheet pans. Place three strips on each greased pan, spacing them well apart.

3. Flatten the dough with the fingers into strips about 3 to 4 inches wide and about (8 to 10 cm wide, 6 mm thick).

4. If required, brush with egg wash.

5. Bake as directed in the formula.

6. After baking, while cookies are still warm, cut each strip into bars about (4.5 cm) wide.

WAFER COOKIES

Wafer cookies are extremely thin and delicate. They are made with a thin batter that is poured or spread onto a baking sheet and baked. Then, while still hot, the wafer is moulded into a variety of shapes. The most popular shapes the tightly rolled cigarette, the curved tuile and the cup-shaped tulipe. Wafer batter is sweet and buttery and is often flavoured with citrus zest or groundnuts.

MACAROON

The earliest recorded macaroon recipes are for the almond meringue variety similar to amaretti, with a crisp crust and a softer interior. They were made from egg whites and almond paste.

The name of the cookie comes from an Italian word meaning paste, *maccarone.* While origins are uncertain, some culinary historians claim that macaroons can be traced to an Italian monastery. Recipes for macaroons (also spelled "mackaroon," "maccaroon" and "mackaroom") appear in recipe books at least as early as 1725 (Robert Smith's Court Cookery, or the Complete English Cook).

Italian Jews later adopted the cookie because it has no flour or leavening (macaroons are leavened by egg whites) and can be enjoyed during the eight-day observation of Passover. It was introduced to other European Jews and became popular as a year-round sweet. Over time, coconut was added to the ground almonds and, in certain recipes, replaced them. Potato starch is also sometimes included in the recipe, to give the macaroons more body.

North American

In North America, the coconut macaroon is the better known variety. Commercially made coconut macaroons are generally dense, moist and sweet, and often dipped in chocolate. Homemade macaroons and varieties produced by smaller bakeries are commonly light and fluffy. Macaroons made with coconuts are often piped out with a star shaped tip, whereas macaroons made with nuts are more likely shaped individually due to the stiffness of the dough. Because of their lack of wheat and leavening ingredients, macaroons are often consumed during Passover in many Jewish homes.

***Coconut macaroon*Types and Makeup Methods**

SHEET COOKIES

Sheet cookies vary so much that it is nearly impossible to give a single procedure for all of them. Some of them are almost like sheet cakes, only denser and richer. They may even be iced like sheet cakes. Others consist of two or three layers added and baked in separate stages. The following procedure is a general guideline only.

1. Spread the cookie mixture into prepared sheet pans. Make sure the thickness is even.

2. If required, add topping or brush with an egg wash.

3. Bake as directed. Cool.

4. Apply icing or topping, if any.

5. Cut into individual squares or rectangles.

PANNING, BAKING, AND COOLING

PREPARING THE PANS

1. Use clean, unwarped pans.

2. Lining the sheets with parchment or silicone paper is fast, and it eliminates the necessity of greasing the pans.

3. A heavily greased pan increases the spread of the cookie. A greased and floured pan decreases spread.

4. Some high-fat cookies can be baked on ungreased pans.

BAKING

1. Most cookies are baked at a relatively high temperature for a short time.

2. Too low a temperature increases spreading and may produce hard, dry, pale cookies.

3. Too high a temperature decreases spreading and may burn the edges or bottoms.

4. Even one minute of over baking can burn cookies, so watch them closely. The heat of the pan continues to bake the cookies even after they are removed from the oven.

5. Doneness is indicated by color. The edges and bottoms should just be turning a light golden color.

6. With some rich dough, burnt bottoms may be a problem. In this case, double-pan the cookies by placing the sheet pan on a second pan of the same size.

COOLING

1. Remove the cookies from the pans while they are still warm, or they may stick.

2. If the cookies are very soft, do not remove them from the pans until they are cool enough and firm enough to handle. Cookies may be soft when hot but become crisp when cool.

3. Do not cool cookies too rapidly or in cold drafts, or they may crack.

4. Cool completely before storing.

Differences between Biscuits and Cookies

S.no

Biscuits

cookies

It contains 50% of fat

It should be thin and flat

It should be dry and crispy

It contains only different flavour (sometime sprinkled some chopped fruits or nuts on top of the sheeted dough)

It should be close and of a crumbly texture

Sheeting process is done

It contains above 70% of fat
It is bigger than biscuits
It should be little soft
Add fruits and nuts
It should be open and of a coarsely texture
Sheeting or piping is done
FUNCTIONS OF INGREDIENTS IN COOKIES
FLOUR

1. **It acts as a binding agent.**
2. **It is the backbone of the baked products.**
3. **It builds structure of the products.**
4. **It holds other ingredients together and they are distributed evenly into the dough.**

SUGAR

1. **It is used as sweetener**
2. **It improves the flavour and taste**
3. **It caramelizes when heated which provide colour**
4. **It gives hard and crunchy texture**
5. **It helps to get even texture**
6. **It gives crispiness**
7. **It keeps the eating qualityFAT**

1. **It provides nutrition and flavour**
2. **It makes the product tender**
3. **It gives crispiness**
4. **It is used for shortening value**
5. **It improves the shelf life**
6. **It helps to form a texture**
7. **It improves the eating quality and taste**

EGGS

1. **It provides structure to the products**
2. **It improves the product taste and flavour**
3. **It gives nutritional value**
4. **It improves the grain and texture**
5. **It combines other ingredients together**

FLAVOUR

1. **It gives flavour**
2. **It improves the taste**

PRINCIPLES INVOLVED IN COOKIES PREPARATION

When making biscuits or cookies always remember the following points:-

1. **Use quality raw materials.**
2. **Measure the ingredients accurately.**
3. **Sieve the dry ingredients like cocoa powder, corn flour, baking powder, soda etc., with flour. It will help to mix evenly into the mixture.**
4. **Should mix ammonia, salt with water.**
5. **If you use butter instead of margarine you should reduce the water quantity given in the formula.**
6. **Beat the eggs before adding into the mixture.**
7. **If you use nuts like cashew nuts and pista you should slightly powder it and mix it into the mixture. It will help to cut the biscuits with cutter.**
8. **Work with finger tips while folding the flour. If over mixed the flour gluten will develop and the biscuit will turn hard.**
9. **Over mixed dough makes rolling or piping much more difficult.**
10. **Chill the dough before sheeting. If it is not possible, give sometime for relaxation.**
11. **Do not use too much of dusting flour.**

12. **Small quantity of dough should be sheeted at a time. After cutting, the remaining scrap dough should be mixed with fresh dough immediately. This will avoid toughness from excessive scrap dough.**
13. **Dough should be sheeted to even thickness. You should give special attention to the center portion during sheeting, because that part is generally thicker than the edges.**
14. **Make a biscuit even in size.**
15. **Use prepared tray. The tray should be cleaned or greased and dusted according to the type.**
16. **When arranging the biscuits on trays leave one inch space between each piece, because the biscuit will spread during baking.**
17. **If garnishing or decoration the biscuit before baking, do it immediately after shaping them, otherwise the dough will dry and the decoration will fall off after baking.**
18. **Use correct temperature and time for baking.**
19. **Wait till it turns to golden yellow colour and then remove the biscuits from the oven. Do not over bake.**
20. **Cool the biscuits slightly and keep them in an airtight container.**
21. **Do not use too much essence. It gives a bitter taste to the products.**
22. **If you are using any topping on the cookie or biscuits like jam, make sure that there is enough space for it to melt and expand.**

IV

Different Types of Paste

Different types of Paste: Short crust, Sweet crust, Rough puff, puff paste, choux paste, Suet paste-preparation, faults and products of the above pastes.

Shortcrust pastry

Shortcrust pastry is a type of pastry often used for the base of a tart, quiche or pie. It does not puff up during baking because it usually contains no leavening agent. It is possible to make shortcrust pastry with self-raising flour, however. Shortcrust pastry can be used to make both sweet and savory pies such as apple pie, quiche, lemon meringue or chicken pie. Many shortcrust pastries are prepared using vegetable shortening, a fat food product that is solid at room temperature, the composition of which lends to creating crumbly, shortcrust-style pastries and pastry crusts.

Proportions

It is based on a "half-fat-to-flour" ratio. Fat (lard, shortening, butter or full-fat margarine) is rubbed into plain flour to create a loose mixture that is then bound using a small amount of ice water, rolled out, then shaped and placed to create the top or bottom of a flan or pie. Ideally, equal amounts of butter and lard are used to make the pastry, ensuring that the ratio of the two fat products is half that of the flour. The butter is employed to give the pastry a rich flavor, whilst the lard ensures optimum texture.

Techniques

In both sweetcrust and shortcrust pastry, care must be taken to ensure that fat and flour are blended thoroughly before liquid is added. This ensures that the flour granules are adequately coated with fat and are less likely to develop gluten and may be achieved with the use of a specialized kitchen utensil called a pastry blender, or through various alternatives, like a pair of table knives held in one hand.

Overworking the dough is also a hazard. Overworking elongates the gluten strands, creating a product that is tough, rather than light and crumbly or flaky.

Types

Pâte à foncer

Pâte à foncer is French shortcrust pastry that includes egg. Egg and butter are worked together with a small quantity of sugar and salt before the flour is drawn into the mixture and cold water added to bind it.

Pâte brisée

This is similar to pâte à foncer, but is lighter and more delicate due to an increased quantity of butter — up to three fifths the quantity of flour.

Sweetcrust pastry

Sweetcrust pastry is made with the addition of sugar, which sweetens the mix and impedes the gluten strands, creating a pastry that breaks up easily in the mouth.

Shortcrust pastry

(sometimes known as medium flakey pastry in the USA) is made from flour; fat, usually lard or butter; water; and salt. The process is quick. The chilled butter or lard is cut into cubes and rubbed into the flour (already sifted and salted) to produce a mixture looking like coarse breadcrumbs. A well is made in this and iced water added little by little and stirred in until the dough coheres and can be formed into a ball. This is wrapped in foil or greaseproof paper and chilled for a short time before being rolled out and used.

Suet crust is the same, but made with suet as the fat. It has a very light texture.

Hot water crust (sometimes called short flake in the USA) has the same ingredients, but the water added is boiling. This causes the fat to melt. The result is a pastry which is strong in both the raw and cooked state, and therefore suitable for use in raised pies (see pie).

Rich shortcrust involves a change in the ingredients. There is more fat in relation to the flour. Egg may be added, and sometimes sugar. The result is relatively soft, crumbly, and tender—and sweet, if sugar has been added. The French *pâte brisée* (meaning broken-textured pastry) is of this type. It is the classic pastry for flans and often has a little sugar, even when used for savoury dishes, but rarely egg. *Pâte sucrée* (sweet pastry) does include egg, and a larger dose of sugar; and it may also be called *pâte sèche* (dry pastry). The Austrian *mürbe Teig* (tender pastry) is a rich shortcrust with egg and sour cream or cream cheese; the latter ingredient gives it a special flavour. The same applies to the rich shortcrust used for *Linzertorte* (see Torte and Kuchen) which includes ground almond as an ingredient. A further variation is found in the rich shortcrust used for the Russian coulibiac, which differs in being made with yeast, which makes it light and puffy. Indeed, it could be held that it really belongs in the next group.

Rough puff, flaky.

Here we have a difference of technique rather than of ingredients. If rich shortcrust pastry is folded and rolled three or four times it becomes what is known as rough puff pastry. The layers of this partly separate and rise during cooking, although not nearly as much as in puff pastry proper. Rough puff is used for quickly made pie crusts. So is flaky pastry (sometimes known as long flake in the USA). It is made from flour with a high proportion of butter, and a little water. A quarter of the butter is added to the flour in the initial stage, resulting in a normal shortcrust pastry. Then the pastry is rolled, dotted with a further quarter of the butter, folded, re-rolled and allowed to rest in a cool place. The procedure is repeated twice more until all the butter is used. This pastry is finely layered with irregular inclusions of butter, giving a light but short texture midway between that of rich shortcrust and puff pastry. French *demi feuilleté* (half-puff) pastry is similar, but the butter left from the original mixing is added in a flat sheet at the first stage, so that the three turns and rolls spread it out more evenly between the layers. Its texture is closer to that of true puff pastry.

puff pastry,

only about one-eighth of the butter is incorporated in the original mixture. The pastry is rolled out. Then the rest of the butter is spread over two-thirds of the area of the sheet of pastry, which is then folded into three in such a way that there are three layers of pastry enclosing two of butter. Folding and rolling is carried out six times in all, with rests between turns. The resulting pastry has 729 layers each separated by a thin smear of butter. Older methods called for folding in two and for nine turns, giving 512 layers. Either way, the pastry rises to a very light, laminated texture, crisp and frail. Puff pastry is used in delicate sweet and savoury articles of many kinds.

Yeast puff pastry is a richer kind, originally a speciality of Vienna and now used to make croissants and similar articles. The dough is made with yeast, milk, and eggs as well as flour and a mixture of butter and lard. Depending on the particular recipe, the dough is given up to four rolls and turns. The combined effect of the rolling and turning and the rise produced by the yeast is to give a pastry as light as normal puff pastry, but with a softer, richer texture and a more interesting flavour.

Choux pastry

is made by melting butter in hot water, adding flour, and cooking the mixture until it is smooth and no longer sticky. Then eggs are beaten in one by one. The raw pastry is very soft, and is usually piped through a forcing bag. When cooked, it rises greatly and has a delicate, spongy texture which finds application in éclairs and similar light delicacies.

Filo pastry is treated separately.

The striking differences in texture between various kinds of pastry have simple causes which lie in the nature of wheat flour and certain kinds of fat. Wheat flour, when kneaded into a plain dough made with water, develops strands of gluten, which are what give an elastic, tough quality to bread. In ordinary pastry, such a texture is undesirable; so a fat or oil is added. This retards the development of the gluten, mainly by physically interposing itself between the grains of flour so that the strands cannot tangle and be drawn out. A hard, solid fat such as lard or suet is most effective here. Lard in particular has a coarse, crystalline structure which makes a highly effective barrier. Butter is less effective, and shortcrust pastry made with butter alone has an inferior texture. If the fat is melted with hot water, or if liquid oil is used, the thin oily layer between the grains offers less obstacle to gluten formation and the resulting pastry is tougher. This is the effect deliberately sought in hot water pastry.

The fact that pastry made with solid fat is stiffer, both when raw and in the early stages of baking, is due simply to the solidity of the fat, and is unconnected with the previous phenomenon.

In puff pastry a certain amount of gluten formation is desirable, but all the strands of gluten must lie in one plane to give strength to the horizontal sheets. Thus the process is one of repeatedly stretching a mixture with only a little fat in it, but whose layers are separated by a barrier of butter. A good deal of air also gets in between the layers and it is partly the expansion of this, and partly the steam formed in cooking, which force the layers apart and make puff pastry rise in such a striking way.

In choux pastry, another notable riser, the preliminary cooking of a flour and fat mixture creates a smooth paste into which air can be beaten during the later stage of adding the eggs, which are themselves even better vehicles for air bubbles. The eggs are added after the cooking stage, simply to avoid hardening them prematurely.

In filo pastry, the gluten is developed to its full extent. The dough used is a mixture of flour and water only, which is thoroughly kneaded and then stretched so that the gluten strands are all horizontal. In this way it resembles a single leaf of puff pastry. When several layers of filo are wrapped around a filling they are brushed with melted butter to separate them, so that the resemblance to puff pastry is increased.

In strudel pastry, the reduction of gluten formation resulting from adding fat and egg to the dough is compensated for by the use of strong, high-gluten bread flour, and by adding a little vinegar to the mixture, which chemically assists the gluten to form.

In flaky, puff, filo, and strudel doughs, where gluten is formed, the process is assisted by giving the dough one or more 'rests' in a cool place. Ideally two hours in a refrigerator is required for each rest. During this time the gluten strands, which have been greatly stressed by the rolling or whichever process is used, draw themselves out a little more as the result of this tension, and thus become not only longer but also slacker. Once the gluten has 'relaxed' in this way, it is easier to stretch it further next time.

Suet Paste For Puddings

Suet paste for puddings is made by mixing chopped suet with flour, and making the whole into a smooth paste with water. The richness of the paste or crust depends upon the quality and quantity of the suet: the rule being:, the more suet the richer the crust. The best kind of suet is the hard beef suet, known as kidney suet. For making a good suet crust the suet must be chopped very fine, (see

No 16) and you must avoid lumps. Good ordinary crust, fairly rich, can be made by mixing one pound of flour to half a pound of suet. When the flour and chopped suet, in the above quantities, have been thoroughly mixed, the suet being rubbed into the flour with the addition of half a salt spoonful of salt, mix with it sufficient water to make it into a smooth paste. Flour a paste-board, and roll it out to the required thickness. For making meat puddings, about a quarter of an inch thick; for fruit puddings, rather less.

For a first-class rich pudding, such as snipe, lark, etc., use three quarters of a pound of the best beef suet to one pound of flour.

For an ordinary good pudding, meat or fruit, for everyday purposes, half a pound of suet to one pound of flour.

For a cheap plain pudding for children, a quarter of a pound of suet to one pound of flour.

Veal suet and mutton suet will make suet puddings. The hard suet from the inside of the loin of mutton will make a very good pudding, but is not equal to beef suet.

V

Icings, Fillings and Glazes

Icings, Fillings and Glazes_ Different types of Icings, Fillings and Glazes and their uses, Chocolate and Sugar Confectionery, Liqueur Chocolate, toffees and boiled sweets, fudges, pulled sugar, blown sugar, pastilles and petit fours.

Icing, also called **frosting** in the United States, is a sweet often creamy glaze made of sugar with a liquid such as water or milk, that is often enriched with ingredients such as butter, egg whites, cream cheese, or flavorings and is used to cover or decorate baked goods, such as cakes or cookies. Elizabeth Raffald documented the first recipe for icing in 1769 in the Experienced English Housekeeper, according to the Food Timeline. However, it was not until 1915 that Mrs. Fred W. Gurney created the first butter cream recipe, and Fannie Farmer followed suit with several more recipes in 1918 and 1923.

Icing can be formed into shapes such as flowers and leaves using a pastry bag. Such decorations are common place on birthday and wedding cakes. Chef's color dye (food coloring) is commonly added to icing mixtures to achieve the desired color. Sprinkles, coloring mist, Edible Image® designs or other decorations are often used on top of icing.

The simplest icing is a glacé icing, containing icing sugar and water. This can be flavored and colored as desired, for example by using lemon juice in place of the water. More complicated icings can be made by beating fat into icing sugar (as in butter cream), by melting fat and sugar together, by using egg whites (as in royal icing), and by adding other ingredients such as glycerin (as in fondant). Some icings can be made from combinations of sugar and cream cheese or sour cream, or by using ground almonds (as in marzipan).

Icing can be applied with a utensil such as a knife or spatula, or it can be applied by drizzling or dipping (see glaze) or by rolling the icing out and draping it over the cake. The method of application largely depends on the type and texture of icing being used. Icing may be used between layers in a cake as a filling, or it may be used to completely or partially cover the outside of a cake or other baked product.

Icing (food)

his cake has an icing made with chocolate and sour cream.

Types - Frosting or Icing, Fillings and Glazes

The basic **frosting or icing recipe** contains butter, sugar, and a liquid such as water or milk. More liquid is added for a glaze. Flavorings such as extracts, fruit zest or juice, and chocolate are often added. Sugar is the most important ingredient in all types of frostings, providing sweetness, flavor, bulk and structure. For richer flavor, unsalted grade A butter is used instead of margarine or shortening, but icings made with shortening will hold up better in warmer environments. For safety, frostings containing **raw eggs should be heated** to certain temperatures to kill any bacteria. Frostings containing egg whites should be whipped with oil-free utensils. Any oil on utensils or in the mixing bowl will prevent the egg whites from whipping into peaks.

If tinting the filling, frosting, etc use restraint. I recommend using gel colors because they are much more subtle than the paste ones, and allow for a greater marginof error. Mix the color a few shades lighter than you want because as it dries, the color will get darker as it sits, especially overnight. Always mix more than you think you'll need of each. It is almost impossible to mix the exact color again if you need more.

Commonly used frostings or icings, fillings and glazes:

DESCRIPTION / CONSISTENCY

HOW MADE

BEST USED FOR / COLORING

STORAGE

SPECIAL INFORMATION

7- MINUTE / BOILED ICING

Marshmallow-like texture, 100% fat free.

ex: **Seven Minute Vanilla Bean Icing Recipe**

Made by warming egg whites, sugar, and a bit of water and beating until it's fluffy and glossy. Substituting light brown sugar for granulated sugar makes sea-foam frosting. Sets quickly.

Most commonly used both between layers and to cover a devil's food cake. / Is pure white and can be tinted to yield pastels.

Best used immediately. Iced cake can be stored at room temperature. Keeps for about 24 hours, and then deflates. Does not freeze well.

Will deflate if mixed with ingredients containing fat such as chocolate or whipped cream.

AMERICAN BUTTERCREAM / CONFECTIONERS' SUGAR ICING

Several styles. Is most popular choice for frosting. Sweet, buttery flavior. Can be slightly gritty. Great for most decorating.

ex: **Tami's or Perfect Buttercream Recipe** or **Tami's or Perfect Buttercream - Not as Sweet Version**

Butter(and/or shortening) and cream or milk are beaten together, and then confectioners' sugar added. Flavored with extracts and chocolate. Can be made thin to stiff consistency, and fluffy or smooth.

Better cream from www.richs.com: whipped butter cream icing used to decorate cakes that store bakeries use.

Use as an frosting and filling. Can be piped for smooth, borders, writing. Most decorations including roses, drop flowers, sweet peas and figure piping. Flowers remain soft enough to be cut with a knife. Use or serve at room temperature. / Yields all colors. Most colors deepen overnight. Some colors may fade sitting in bright light.

Icing can be refrigerated in an airtight container for 2 weeks or frozen. Iced cake can be stored at cool side of room temperature for 2-3 days.

Does not hold up well in warm weather, unless shortening is used. Jams and ganache are always great alternatives to butter cream fillings and hold-up well in warm weather.

BUTTERCREAM - FRENCH

Is very rich.

ex: **Neoclassic French Buttercream Recipe**

Uses egg yolks (or whole eggs) and is made the same way as Italian meringue.

Filling and frosting.

Needs refrigeration

Due to the egg yolks, this butter cream is very perishable and should be kept refrigerated.

BUTTERCREAM - MERINGUE ITALIAN (MOUSSELINE) AND SWISS

Fluffy and buttery. Medium to thick consistency.

exs: **Italian Meringue or Mousseline Buttercream Recipe (IMBC)** and

Swiss Meringue Buttercream Recipe (SMBC)

Both use only egg whites, but differences are how they are made. Italian: Hot sugar syrup is added to already whipped egg whites. Swiss: The whites and sugar are mixed together over heat and whipped. Then, cooled before the butter and flavoring are added. This type of butter cream is the simplest.

Frosting and filling on cake. Suggest making a filling dam if used as a filling otherwise may squish from cake. / Yields pastel colors.

Needs refrigeration.

Italian holds up well in warm weather (75 degrees plus) and is more dependable. Swiss tends to deflate a little quicker and doesn't hold up as well in warm environments.

BUTTERCREAM - ROLLED

Sweet. Similar to fondant.

ex: **Rolled Buttercream Recipe**

Made from stiff American butter cream.

Dough-like consistency that is rolled out before applied to cake.

Covering cakes and cookies / Can be tinted; see butter cream

Same as American Buttercream

Is very soft and can be hard to work with.

CANDY CLAY

Edible and sweet. Texture like Play Doh. Also makes a delicious chocolate candy.

ex: **Easy Candy Clay or Chocolate Plastic from Candy Melts Recipe**

Can be made with a mixture of heated Candy Melts and corn syrup. Dough-like consistency that is rolled out before applied to cake.

Covering cakes, hand-molding and decorating. Mix with gum paste for more strength / Yields all colors if using white candy melts.

After making, handles best if hardened overnight. Several weeks at room temperature in a well-sealed container.

Will be very hard at the start; knead a small portion at a time until workable.

CITRUS (LEMON) CURD

A conserve or custard with a thick consistency. Tart flavor.

ex: **Fresh Lemon Curd Recipe**

Made with lemons and butter and eggs and sugar, and cooked on the stovetop. Can be purchased ready-made.

Spread on bread or cakes. Used as a filling. Fold in with whipped cream or pastry cream.

Keep refrigerated.

Needs refrigeration.

CREAM CHEESE

Slightly tangy, but can be sweet. Thick and creamy. Thin to medium consistency. Classic pairing for American oil cakes such as carrot and spice cakes.

ex: **Cream Cheese Buttercream Frosting Recipe**

Cream cheese and butter are beaten together with confectioners‘ sugar and a flavoring such as vanilla extract.

Cream cheese frostings get really soft quickly after you take them out of the fridge. Look for Handy Pac cream cheese frosting and filling available online or in cake supply stores.

Filling and frosting cakes. / Colors to pastels.

Iced cake must be refrigerated.

Handy Pac cream cheese is shelf stable vs. using the actual cream cheese which needs to be refrigerated.

To not mar the frosted cake's surface when refrigerating, let it harden first in the refrigerator, then cover with plastic wrap. When you take it from the refrigerator, immediately remove plastic wrap and let it sit to soften before serving.

CUSTARD OR PUDDINGS

Different varieties. Pastry cream or Citrus curd(custards, cooked) or mousse(pudding, not cooked). Thick, smooth and creamy.

exs: **Pastry Cream Tutorial**

and

Fresh Lemon Curd Recipe

and

White Chocolate Raspberry Mousse Recipe

Custard(pastry cream) thickened with flour or cornstarch. See Citrus curd.

Fruit puree or flavored base(mousse) folded in with whipped cream or beaten egg whites.

Fillings used alone. A small amount can be folded into whipped cream to flavor it.

Must remain refrigerated.

Highly perishable. Needs refrigeration.

FONDANT - ROLLED

Used for its special look on wedding cakes. Rich, sweet flavor. Covers with a perfectly smooth, matte finish. Does not dry as hard as royal icing and stays semi-soft. Seals in freshness and moisture.

exs: **Rolled Fondant Recipe**

and

Marshmallow Fondant Recipe (MMF)

Combination of sugar and vegetable shortening that makes a thick white dough-like substance, and then rolled out. Can be made with marshmallows. Knead in flavor and color of your choice. Can be purchased ready-made.

Rolled out and used as a cake covering. Use on any firm butter, pound or fruit cake. Even on cookies. Can be cut-out and used as decorations. / Yields pastel to deep colors. But, does not have much flavor.

The best choice for outdoor events. Excess can be stored 2 months in an airtight container. Can refrigerate but must take steps to rid of condensation from cake.

Holds up well in hot weather but, will soften in warm or humid weather. Prior to applying, cake must be covered in apricot glaze, buttercream icing or marzipan so fondant will adhere.

FONDANT - POURED

Very sweet flavor. Covers cakes with perfectly smooth, satiny iced surface. Seals in freshness.

ex: **Poured Fondant for Cakes and Cookies Recipe**

and

Simple Fondant Glaze Recipe

Pours and dries to a semi-hard, smooth surface.

All cakes, petit fours and cookies. / Yileds pastels.

Excess may be refrigerated, reheated and poured again

Will soften in warm, humid weather.

GANACHE

Is a French term. Dark: decadent, rich, and very, very chocolatey. White: Rich velvety taste - a little more complex flavor than a buttercream. Can be glaze, whipped or smooth.

exs: **Poured and Whipped Ganache Tutorial**
and
Simple Chocolate Ganache Recipe, Step-by-Step

This is a rich emulsified mixture of chocolate and cream. Buttercream consistency can be made by whipping soft butter into its base, resulting in *ganache beurre.*

Glaze. filling and/or frosting: whipped or smooth / Natural color is dark to medium brown or white. Can be flavored(oil-based). White can also be tinted(oil-based)

Needs refrigeration after 2 to 3 days at room temperature, 2 weeks refrigerated and 6 months frozen. Keep excess with a piece of plastic wrap pushed on its surface.

The better the chocolate used, the better the ganache. Good for warm (not hot) weather.

GLAZES

Simple and sugary. Smooth: thick or thin.
ex: **Chocolate Glaze Recipe**

GUM PASTE

Dough-like. Thick and malleable.
ex: **Gumpase or Tylose Gum Paste Recipe**

Gum based paste with a stiffening agent. Can be purchased ready-made.

Cutting molding and modeling decorations. / Deep to pastel colors.

Excess can be stored 2 months in an airtight container. Best not refrigerated. Do not freeze.

Decorations will survive warm days, but is susceptible to extreme heat and humidity where it will soften.

JAMS AND JELLIES

ex: **Italian Strawberry Tart or Crostata di Fragole Tutorial**
and
Ultimate Fresh Strawberry Butter Cake Recipe (UFSBC)

Can purchase ready-made: stir it to soften, or heat with small amount of liquid if it's too thick, and strain to remove the seeds.

Used as a filling alone or in combination with other fillings such as buttercream or ganache.

Refrigerate after opening. Is not perishable if used as a filling.

Great for warm or hot weather. But, filled cakes should be stored in refrigerator for long-term storage to prevent mold.

MARZIPAN

is used similarly to rolled fondant because it gives a smooth look. It has a delicious and unique almond flavor.

ex: **Marzipan Recipe**

Marzipan is made of almond paste. Can purchase ready-made. Dough-like consistency that is rolled out before applied to cake. Is stretchy. Stays semi-soft on cakes.

Rolled out and used as a cake or cookie covering, and then, covered with a sugar icing, such as fondant or buttercream. Can be used to mold flowers and other decorations that are then placed on a cake or served alone. / Is off-white and can used in its natural color or be tinted.

Keep almond paste well covered and refrigerated, since it contains almonds which can go rancid.

Holds up well in warm weather.

MERINGUE

Pure white fluffy beaten egg whites.

ex: **How To Beating Techniques for Meringue**

Is made from beating egg whites with sugar. There are many types depending on the ratio of its ingredients.

Used for covering pies, cakes and Baked Alaska. Can be piped.

Does not need refrigeration. Becomes sticky when refrigerated.

Can weep after storage, even for a day or two. Refrigeration speeds up the weeping process.

ROYAL ICING

Pure white, sticky icing that dries to a hard finish.

ex: **Royal Icing Master Recipe**

Heavy paste of egg whites and confectioners' sugar beaten with a little vinegar or lemon juice. Can be made in different consistencies.

Used for general piping or delicate work such as elaborate "string" decorations. Decorating cookies and gingerbread houses. / Tints to pastel to dark colors.

Does not need refrigeration. Air-dried decorations last for months.

Will soften when placed on butter or fat based frostings.

SIMPLE SUGAR SYRUPS

Simple and sugary.

ex: **Basic Simple Sugar Syrup Recipe with Flavor Variations**

Made from confectioners' sugar and water, and then cooked. Can be flavored which should complement or match the flavors of the cake.

Brushed on drier cake layers to moisten them, such as genoise. Syrup is popular in wedding cakes and other large projects that must be made in multiple stages; keeps it tasting fresh and moist longer. Syrup is not usually used alone as a filling; the layers are brushed with syrup and then another filling, such as jam or buttercream, is spread on top.

Keep excess refrigerated. Cakes that are moistened with sugar syrups can mold easily.

Holds up well in warm weather, but gets sticky when humid. Bowls/utensils must be grease-free. Cover icing with damp cloth while working, to prevent crusting.

WHIPPED CREAM

Creamy, delicate sweetness. Perishable.

exs: **Whipped Cream Tutorial**

and

Stabilized Whipped Cream Recipe

Whipping cream beaten with sugar. Can be flavored. Stabilized for longer life with gelatin.

Can be used as a filling and frosting. Can be piped to form soft decorations. /Tints in pastel colors.

Must remain refrigerated.

Use immediately because deflates readily. Iced cake must be refrigerated. Texture remains soft on decorated cake.

Cacao beans

Early 19th century recipes for chocolate liqueur featured whole cocoa beans. A basic modern recipe for making chocolate liqueur at home lists the ingredients chocolate extract, vanilla extract, vodka, and simple syrup. To keep the chocolate extract in suspension and make the liqueur thicker, glycerine may be added. In its purest form, chocolate liqueur is clear; coloring may be added. Recipes for home-made chocolate liqueurs may also include raw eggs as an ingredient, presenting a risk of salmonellosis. Reasonable safety may be achieved by combining the eggs with the alcohol before other ingredients

Uses of Chocolate liqueur

Chocolate liqueur can be consumed straight, as an after dinner drink rather than as aperitif. It is used in mixed drinks and in desserts, especially in dessert sauces, cakes, and truffles. A food writer notes that many recipes for chocolate truffle add a small amount of chocolate liqueur to melted chocolate, and warns that adding the liqueur often causes the chocolate to seize. One of the more unusual uses is in chocolate rolled fondant. several people noted the wines had a flavor of chocolate liqueur and were fakes. Wine and chocolate are a classic flavor pairing, and this is reflected in some cocktails that combine a strong red wine with a dash of chocolate liqueur.

Hard candy/boiled sweet

Alternative name(s)

Boiled sweet

Details

Type

Confectionery

Main ingredient(s)

Syrup (sucrose, glucose, or fructose) or isomalt, citric acid, food colouring, flavouring

Variations

Many (such as candy cane or lollipop)

A **hard candy**, or **boiled sweet**, is a candy prepared from one or more syrups boiled to a temperature of 149 °C (300 °F). After a syrup boiled to this temperature cools, it is called hard candy, since it becomes stiff and brittle as it approaches room temperature. Hard candy recipes variously call for syrups of sucrose, glucose, or fructose.

Once the syrup blend reaches the target temperature, the confectioner removes it from the heat source, and may add citric acid, food dye, and some flavouring, such as a plant extract, essential oil, or flavorant. One might then pour the syrup concoction (which is now very viscous) into a mold or tray to cool. When the syrup is cool enough to handle, one can fold, roll, and mold it into the shapes desired.

Hard candies and throat lozenges prepared without sugar employ isomalt as a sugar substitute, and are sweetened further by the addition of an artificial sweetener, such as aspartame, or a sugar alcohol, such as xylitol.

Among the many hard candy varieties are stick candy (such as the candy cane), the lollipop, the aniseed twist, and the *bêtises de Cambrai*.

Pulled Sugar

For a cake or dessert centerpiece, there is nothing more elegant and impressive than edible decorations. Sugar is a clay, the baker a sculptor. Sugar can be formed into just about any shape you can imagine. When liquefied and heated, it becomes pliable enough for a few moments to be sculpted into objects, ribbons and decorations. The process of molding sugar is known as pulling, as you pull the molten sugar in order to form smooth lines that then harden into a brittle sugar sculpture1 1/4 cups sugar

- 100 ml water
- food dye

Show (2) More

- Bring to boil 1 1/4 cups sugar and 100 ml of water over high heat. Attach a candy thermometer to the side of the pot. Once it reaches boiling point, stir in 1 tsp. of lemon juice and food coloring of your choice. Watch the thermometer carefully until it reads 298 degrees Fahrenheit. Let the mixture reach this temperature or it will not properly harden when cooled. The trick to candy making is bringing it to peak at a high temperature. If you do not use a thermometer, you risk gooey candy.
- Pour the boiling candy syrup onto a silicone mat. You can use a piece of parchment paper, but make sure the paper sticks to the counter. Hold it down with tape or weights. Do not use wax paper, which will melt and stick to your candy. Put on a pair of pastry gloves or kitchen sink gloves to keep from burning yourself once you begin to pull.
- Allow the sugar to cool briefly (less than a minute), only so it is solid yet bendable. If you let it sit for more than a minute it will harden and you will have a sheet of sugar, perhaps pretty for a cake plate, but not for sugar pulling purposes.
- Begin to pull. Fold the sugar back and forth to get the feel of it, and then cut off small pieces and begin to stretch, pull and twirl the sugar into any form you desire. You must work quickly. You can use tools such as dowels to help you create ribbon curls, or bend it in droplets to make flowers.
- Reheat if the sugar cools before you finish. Place the sugar under a heat lamp or in a pot over low heat on the stove or in the oven. Do not let it melt, or you will have caramel. Let it warm enough only so that it is pliable again, and then repeat the pulling of small pieces into ribbons or shapes.

Blown Sugar Glass

Sugar can be heated and manipulated to replicate blown glass.

Sugar glass, also known as pulled sugar, is a technique that allows sugar to be manipulated into different shapes while keeping a glassy look. Pulled sugar can be blown like real glass to make round objects. This process uses high temperatures, so it's important to make sure the sugar is cooled before touching it with your hands.

- 1 cup sugar
- 1 cup corn syrup
- 2 drops tartaric acid

- Pour 1 cup of sugar and 1 cup of corn syrup into a pot. Stir to mix them well.
- Add two drops of tartaric acid to the pot.
- Put the pot on the stove and bring the temperature to 320 degrees F.
- Wait for the sugar to start boiling and turn off the heat.
- Pour the boiling sugar onto a piece of parchment paper.
- Let the sugar cool completely on the paper.
- Put a heating lamp over the parchment paper, and turn it on once the sugar has cooled completely. This will make it easy to shape.
- Roll the sugar into a clump and put it on the nozzle of the hand pump.
- Pump air into the sugar; the sugar should blow like a bubble.
- Play around with the hand pump and sugar until you get a shape you like.
- Use the fan to cool the sugar once you have a shape you want.

Pastilles are a type of candy or medicinal pill made of a thick liquid that has been solidified and is meant to be consumed by light chewing and allowing it to dissolve in the mouth. They are also used to describe certain forms of incense.A pastille is also known as a "troche", or a medicated lozenge that dissolves like candy.

Origins

Pastilles were originally a pill-shaped lump of compressed herbs, which was burnt to release its medicinal properties. References to the burning of medicinal pastilles include the short story "Birthmark" by Nathaniel Hawthorne, the poem "The Laboratory" by Robert Browning, and the novel Jane Eyre by Charlotte Brontë. They are also mentioned in the novel McTeague by Frank Norris, when the title character's wife burns them to mask an unpleasant odor in the couple's rooms. They were also widely used during the eighteenth century in Western cultures to take herbal curatives and medicines, which eventually were developed into candies.

Production

Pastilles are made by pouring a thick liquid into a powdered, sugared, or waxed mold and then allowing the liquid to set and dry. The substances contained in the dried liquid are slowly released when chewed and allowed to dissolve in the mouth. The substances are then absorbed by the mucous membranes of the oral cavity or in the lower gastro-intestinal tracts. Various substances, be they of medicinal nature or for flavour can be put into pastille forms.

Due to the oily nature of these active substances (essential oils, tinctures and extracts), pastilles are usually based on a mixtures of starch and gum Arabic, which emulsifies the substance and binds them in a hydrocolloidal matrix. The starch and gum also reduces the rate in which the pastille dissolves and moderates the amount of active substances delivered at a time. Gum Arabic also hardens the pastilles and makes them more sturdy in storage and transport.

Types

Well known pastille type candies include:

- Jujube

- Rowntree's Fruit Pastilles, small round sweets
- Vichy Pastilles, octagonal candy pastilles
- Wine gum
- Grether's Pastilles
- Pastiglie Leone, Herbal digestives and candy pastilles

History

Petits fours were traditionally made during the cooling process of coal-powered brick ovens in the 18th century. This was due to coal's high burning temperature, relative to wood, and its expense at the time. Wasting the heat produced was not an option.

Petit four

An assortment of petits fours

French assortment of petits fours

A **petit four** (plural: **petits fours**) is a small confectionery generally eaten at the end of a meal (e.g., with coffee) or served as part of dessert. The name is from the French*petit four* (French pronunciation: meaning "small oven".

There are two different categories of petits fours. *Petits fours secs* (*sec* meaning "dry") include a variety of small desserts, such as special dainty biscuits, baked meringues, macaroons, and puff pastries. *Petits fours glacés* (*glacé* meaning "iced") are iced or decorated in some way, such as tiny cakes covered in fondant or glacé icing, small éclairs, and tartlets. In a French patisserie, assorted small desserts are usually called mignardises, while hard, buttery biscuits are called petit fours.

There are also *petits fours salés* (*salé* meaning "salted" or "savoury"), which are bite-sized salted appetizers usually served as part of cocktail parties or buffets.

9 798889 517849

Printed by Libri Plureos GmbH in Hamburg,
Germany